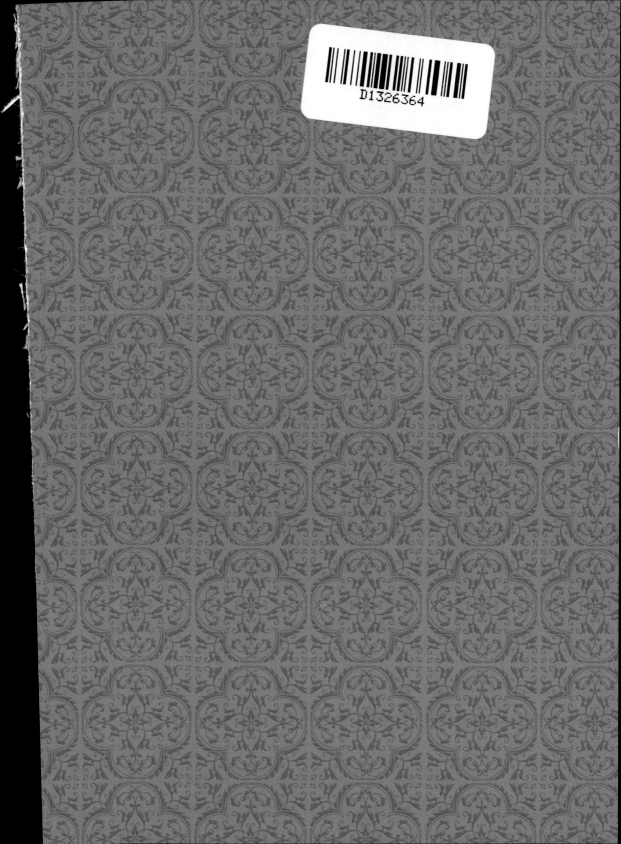

VICTORIAN PHARMACY

VICTORIAN PHARMACY

REDISCOVERING FORGOTTEN REMEDIES AND RECIPES

JANE EASTOE
FOREWORD BY RUTH GOODMAN

PAVILION

A Note on the Remedies

*T*his book contains information on historical techniques, methods and remedies used during the Victorian period. Where remedies are reproduced they must be considered in the context of their original publication.

☠ Remedies in the main text marked with skull and crossbones contain harmful and dangerous ingredients and should not be attempted under any circumstances. They illustrate some of the techniques, methods and pharmaceutical ideas prevalent in the Victorian period and are included for historical interest only.

🥄 Recipes set out in the sidebars and identified with a spoon illustrate the types of Victorian remedies that may still be relevant today. They are included purely for entertainment purposes and may be attempted, but only and entirely at the reader's own risk. Please be aware that some of the ingredients may cause adverse reactions and you are advised to consult a competent professional before attempting them. By way of example, they may react with prescription drugs and other medications as well as affecting pre-existing medical conditions. They are not a replacement for professional treatment or advice and readers are always advised to seek professional advice before using herbal remedies.

The Publishers make no warranties or representations to the completeness, accuracy, reliability or suitability of such ingredients, recipes or remedies and exclude liability arising from reliance on such information to the fullest extent of the law.

CONTENTS

FOREWORD

When I was first asked if I would be involved in making a programme about Victorian pharmacy I jumped at the chance. It is such a fascinating subject involving so many of the nitty gritty practicalities of everyday life. Working with Nick and Tom I was to get a chance to cast a light on the shadowy worlds of arsenic poisoning, medicated toilet paper and mystery potions. Everyone used pharmacists for something; it would be a window into the lives of society ladies as well as desperate single mothers, from the young man with acne hoping to improve his courting chances to his father's worries about his bald spot, from the terror of cholera to the violence of the 'cures'.

Jane Eastoe's book gives us a wonderful view into the daily realities of Victorian living and dying. The history of medicine as it is taught in schools is all about the great experimental advances, the march of understanding, the professional and learned. And yes, they are definitely there, the 'heroes', the discoveries. But scratch the surface and there is so much more than that. It is also a history of cosmetics, contraception, exotic plants, chemistry, advertising, mistakes and dishonesty, food, the battle of the sexes, disease and of fear.

The stories twist and turn through all areas of human existence, some very surprising. Who would have thought that my journey would involve making condoms out of sheep guts, burning my nose linings with perfume or being doused in freezing cold water? Nor that so many working class children died of heroin and opium addiction. I was amazed and heartened at how much female involvement there had always been in pharmacy and have emerged with a genuine respect for the men and women who achieved so much in just 60 years.

As you read I am sure, like me, you will find many echoes with your own experience or family stories. Perhaps even products or procedures that you still use today. Victorian pharmacy in practise is not so long ago.

RUTH GOODMAN

INTRODUCTION

'I never read a patent medicine advertisement
without being impelled to the conclusion that
I am suffering from the particular disease therein
dealt with in its most virulent form.'

JEROME K JEROME, *THREE MEN IN A BOAT*

This is the story of consumer medicine, a social revolution that brought healthcare within everyone's reach and brought medical science to every high street in the country, along with family remedies and traditional folklore.

In 1837, at the start of Queen Victoria's reign, medical understanding was much as it had been for centuries. The same was true for its provision and treatment. High street healthcare, however, was emerging, and from humble, herbal beginnings it spawned a new medical industry. By the end of the nineteenth century, the Victorian pharmacy, with its massive stock range, had developed. Recognisable as the ancestor of the modern high-street chemist, it treated every conceivable illness with the most up-to-date remedies inspired by the new sciences of the age.

More than anything, this is the human story of how healthcare was transformed. In *Victorian Pharmacy*, we look at the diseases that haunted everyday life and the bizarre treatments prescribed. This primitive healthcare was exacerbated by the lack of any welfare state provision. It is shocking to learn that, until comparatively recently, a visit to a doctor was an unaffordable luxury for most people.

It was into this arena that the pharmacist, and the chemist and druggist, made an entry. These enterprising men sought to make a business out of herbal cures and readily accessible medicines, thus transforming our healthcare provision. Their natural curiosity led to a greater understanding of the cause and treatment of illness. Moreover, they were natural inventors, with a problem-solving approach that led to the development of all manner of useful sundries we now take for granted. They opened up the market for toiletries, cosmetics and specialist cleaning products, and brought us the likes of Bovril and Bird's Custard Powder.

Over the course of Queen Victoria's reign, the dispensing of medicines moved from being an unregulated profession, dominated by quacks and their phoney cures, to one that was guided by education and rules of good practice. And this was a profession that needed regulating, as physician and educator Peter Mere Latham observed, 'Poisons and medicine are oftentimes the same substance given with different intents.' Off-the-shelf medicines contained a list of ingredients that read like a drug pusher's catalogue: opium, cocaine and cannabis were all used with gay abandon.

Chemists worked long hours and provided their customers with a service that was second to none. Whatever was needed, they would attempt to supply: wart cures, sealing wax, anti-hysteric mixtures, gunpowder, anti-venereal pills, curry powder, pig pills, travel ink and rose nipple cream. They powdered, mixed, diluted, brewed, cooked, devised and advised for all they were worth. Some made fortunes, but some made terrible errors that had devastating consequences.

Many familiar products can be traced back to nineteenth-century formulas; kaolin and morphine mixture, Epsom salts and Bay Rhum are still used today. In *Victorian Pharmacy*, we include original recipes of the day, just as they are found in exquisite, handwritten receipt books. Treatments for everything from baldness to bad breath can be found within their battered covers. The most popular pages are pockmarked with splashes – like favourite recipes in a cookery book.

The recipes are printed as they were written down, using a range of weights and measures and apothecary symbols. Like a magician's book of spells, some recipes are almost impenetrable; even the modern pharmacist finds them tough to decipher. Nonetheless they make a riveting read. Many of the ingredients listed are impossible to buy over the counter today: namely, arsenic, opium and asbestos. We therefore feel confident to print them, on the understanding that no one will be able to gather the basic ingredients required for some of the more *potent* cocktails. Other recipes can safely be made at home: traditional beef tea, sprain oil, a bread poultice or hair pomade.

However, a word of caution should be sounded: any medication can be dangerous in untrained hands, even the herbal ones. It is worth noting that a new law comes into force in 2011 regulating the sale of herbal remedies. This is because 'herbal' does not necessarily mean 'benign' and herbal products can interact with prescribed medication. Due caution should be exercised when using any homemade medications.

CHAPTER I

—— ✦ ——

PUBLIC HEALTH

'A Short History of Medicine:

2000 BC: Here, eat this root.

AD 1000: That root is heathen, say this prayer.

1850: That prayer is superstition, drink this potion.

1940: That potion is snake oil, swallow this pill.

1985: That pill is ineffective, take this antibiotic.

2000: That antibiotic is artificial. Here, eat this root.'

AUTHOR UNKNOWN

At the start of Queen Victoria's reign, the public had long been in the habit of self-medicating. This was partly because of the scarcity of public health provision, but principally because most people simply did not have the pennies to spare on physicians or apothecaries. Many people, notably the working class, had a deep mistrust of physicians, whose cures were often as bad, if not worse, than the original problem. Illnesses were managed rather than cured, and it was not until the end of the nineteenth century that real advances were made in the understanding of the causes of ill health, as well as its management and treatment.

Medical thinking was still dominated by the theories of Hippocrates (460–*c.*370 BC). He suggested that illness was caused by an imbalance in the four *humors* – blood, phlegm, black bile and yellow bile. This approach began

The book of Pharmaceutical Formulas, *essentially a recipe book for pharmacists, detailed all manner of preparations from household and domestic requisites through to medicinal preparations and beverages.* ☞

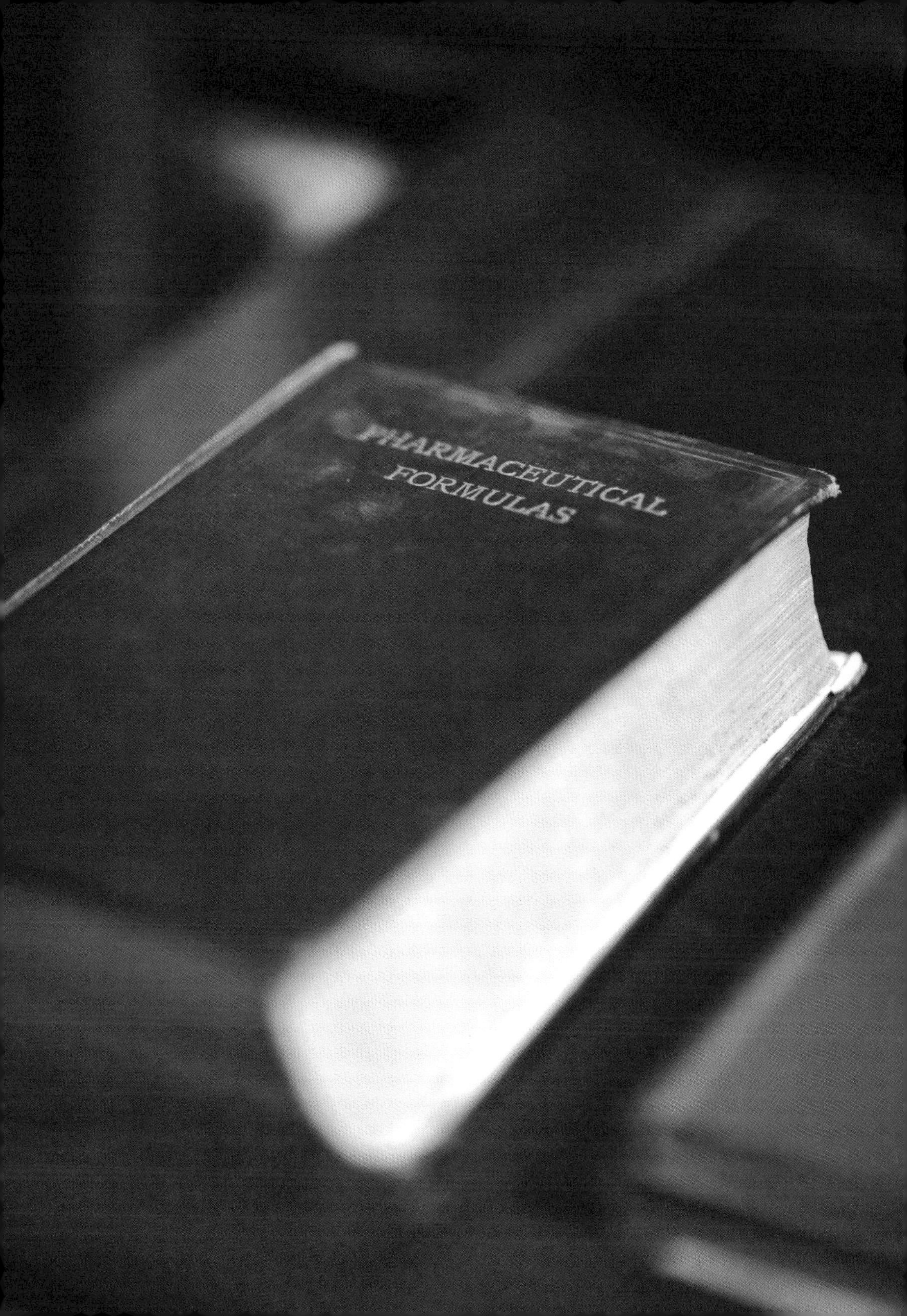
PHARMACEUTICAL
FORMULAS

to be revised only after 1860. Treatments to 'rebalance the humours' and clear the 'miasma of bad air' were vigorous – and not for the faint-hearted.

The principal therapy was blood-letting, but purging and laxative treatments were popular, as were enemas and blistering plasters. The latter were applied to various parts of the body with the intent of causing irritation to the skin; it was common, for example, to fix them behind the ears as a means of alleviating toothache. Medicines and ointments frequently contained highly toxic substances such as antimony, mercury and arsenic. These torturous therapies were commonplace and left patients debilitated or created an addiction. Napoleon Bonaparte (1769–1821) remarked that medicine is 'a collection of uncertain prescriptions the results of which, taken collectively, are more fatal than useful to mankind.'

☠ *Blistering Ointment* ☠

Cantharides in coarse powder 600 grammes
Powdered euphorbium 200 grammes
Black pitch and yellow resin, of each 400 grammes
Yellow wax 300 grammes
Olive oil 1000 grammes

Mix the wax, pitch and resin at a gentle heat; add the oil, constantly stirring; strain through cloth. Put the cantharides and the euphorbium in the vessel and damp with water. Add, little by little, half the resinous mixture, and heat to evaporate the water. Then add the rest of the mixture; heat for a few seconds; withdraw from the fire, and stir well till quite cold.

THE CITIES AND DISEASE

The living conditions in Victorian Britain gave rise to many of the underlying health problems. Of particular significance was the huge shift from rural to urban life. In 1801, only one-fifth of the population lived in towns and cities; by

1850, the figure had risen to approximately half of the population; and by 1901, the ratio had shifted again with four-fifths residing in urban environments. Towns and cities offered employment and escape from rural poverty, but conditions were shocking.

Rapid urban development had been unregu-lated, and the ramshackle, severely overcrowded housing left inhabitants more susceptible to infectious diseases. Access to fresh water was limited, with water companies providing a supply only two to three times a week for just a few hours at any one time. This was a situation that did not improve until halfway through Victoria's reign: it was not until 1870 that a continuous supply of water was made available to Londoners for the first time, though for the majority of people this still meant using a street pump.

Refuse was either stored in the home or left in piles for the scavengers' cart to collect. The dustbin did not make an appearance in Britain until after 1900.

As well as being littered with rubbish, the streets were full of horse manure, so there were flies everywhere in summer. The removal of horse manure was almost as big a problem as that of human waste. Indeed, the management of human sewage was primitive: latrines and cesspits were common, and in the towns and cities a night soil collector made the rounds for those who used only pails. Tons and tons of human waste were removed from the city and despatched to the countryside by boat or train, where it was spread on the fields, thus neatly extending the range of waterborne diseases.

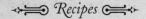

Recipes

Lemon Wash Balls

A lovely lemon-scented soap for handwashing clothing.

Cut 6 lbs of soap into very small pieces; melt it into a pint of water in which 6 lemons have been boiled. When melted, withdraw the soap from the fire and add 3 lbs of powdered starch and a little essence of lemon; knead the whole into a paste and form into balls of the required size.

The first public water closets were seen at The Great Exhibition at Crystal Palace in 1851. To use them, you had to spend a penny – hence the phrase. Theoretically, flush toilets resolved the sewage dilemma, albeit for only the fortunate few. But the disposal of flushed waste was no more ethical; it was pumped into the sewer, and then directed straight into the nearest river – the source of drinking water.

As a result, drinking water was often spoiled by human waste. Both cholera and typhoid, waterborne diseases, were transmitted through contaminated faeces – a fact that was not recognised until the 1850s. Legislation to improve London's water supply was implemented in 1855, and for the first time water was drawn from outside the city and filtered.

The government was forced to take further action after the Great Stink of 1858. In an unusually hot summer, the River Thames and its tributaries overflowed with raw sewage, creating an unbearable stench. The following year, the civil engineer Sir Joseph Bazalgette (1819–1891) started work on the construction of the central London sewage system. The rest of the country followed London's lead to improve water quality, at least in the towns, after 1870.

MALNOURISHMENT AND POLLUTION

But if water supplies and water quality are not what we are used to today, neither was the food. There was little legislation to control the sale of consumables: meat was often rotten and foodstuffs contaminated with dangerous additives as manufacturers competed to produce the cheapest goods. Bakers added alum or chalk to their flour, and mashed potatoes, plaster of Paris or sawdust to increase the weight of their loaves. Brewers added bitter substances, such as strychnine, to their beer to improve taste and save on the cost of hops. People developed a taste for adulterated food, and even principled purveyors were forced to adopt less upright practices because consumers complained that their food didn't 'taste right' without the additives. Legislative controls were not implemented until the Food, Drink and Drugs Act of 1872.

Many working class families were therefore malnourished. Women and children suffered the worst with a diet comprising of bread, margarine and tea with sugar. A survey conducted by Charles Booth over a period of 17 years, and published in 1889, revealed that 35 per cent of London's population lived in abject poverty. Surveys from other cities revealed much the same picture. The memoir *Mrs John Brown: 1847–1935* describes a typical tragedy from the late 1800s:

> *In the bed was a young woman, wan and dazed. She was holding a week-old baby to her empty breast. It was so pitiful I did not know what to say. 'I thought there were two children.' 'There was three days ago,' the woman said. 'Show her, Jem.' The man got up heavily and opened the bottom drawer of a rickety chest, and there lay a little dead child of about two. I gasped. He said, 'We be waiting for the parish to come and bury her.' The mother said, 'We couldn't put her upstairs, alone, in the empty room.' I stood still, sobbing, but the parents shed no tears, nor said a word, except when Jem closed the drawer. 'She were a nice little lass, she were,' he said.*

Pollution was a further problem. The air in towns and cities was heavy with smoke from coal fires, which provided the only means of cooking, hot water and heating. It has been estimated that about two-and-a-half million tons of soot were produced annually by domestic consumption alone. This made day-to-day life squalid and dirty for most people, no matter how hard they might try to keep up appearances. More importantly, the soot contributed to the famous London fogs, or London Peculiars, where visibility was reduced to a couple of feet. They were not, however, limited to the capital; towns all over Britain were plagued by them. The fog was thick and brownish yellow in colour, with a sulphurous, sooty, smoky smell. Unlike most fogs, they did not diminish as the sun rose, but became thicker. Horse-drawn coaches and omnibuses had to be led by men carrying torches to warn of their approach.

The respiratory diseases that followed were a major source of ill-health and death. In December 1873, the *Medical Times and Gazette* described a recent fog as 'one of the most disastrous this generation has known. … To persons with cardiac and respiratory disease it has in numerous instances proved fatal.'

The fogs would not abate until the 1960s. Indeed, the last of the great London fogs went on for four days in December 1952, and is estimated to have killed 4000 people.

This air pollution was also implicated in the high incidence of rickets. Children were more susceptible to this nutritional disease, because thick pollution reduces exposure to sunlight. Rickets was first noted in Britain back in the 1600s, but by the nineteenth century it was widespread. The disease causes softening of the bones, leading to fractures and deformity. A survey undertaken by the British Medical Association in the 1880s revealed a sharp difference between the high incidence of rickets in the urban centres and its virtual absence from small towns, villages and the countryside.

Curiously, bread was implicated. The incidence of rickets was higher in the smoky south because coal was expensive, meaning that it was cheaper for people to buy their bread. Commercially prepared bread was commonly adulterated with alum, an ingredient believed to increase susceptibility to rickets. In the smoky north, where bread was home-baked, children were less susceptible to the disease.

SELF-HELP

In the second quarter of the nineteenth century, it began to dawn on doctors and scientists that this devastating combination of environmental problems was the root cause of many epidemics.

Progress was slow, however, and the sick faced a dilemma: to bankrupt themselves consulting a qualified physician or apothecary, who anyway had little real understanding of disease; or to consult a chemist and druggist for a fraction of the price. For most of the nineteenth century, the chemist and druggist, or pharmacist, was the main source of medical provision for poor and rich alike.

Mrs Beeton's Book of Household Management, first published in 1859, gives some idea of the lengths to which the ordinary housewife was prepared to go when it comes to First Aid. She was advised to keep the following items at home in case of emergencies:

A LONDON FOG.—DRAWN BY DUNCAN.

The London Illustrated News *of 1847 reveals the severity of the thick, sulphurous fogs which caused many deaths.*

Antimonial Wine, Antimonial Powder, Blister Compound, Blue Pill, Calomel, Carbonate of Potash, Compound Iron Pills, Nitre, Oil of Turpentine, Opium (powdered), Laudanum, Sal-Ammoniac, Senna Leaves, Soap Liniment, Opoldeldoc, Sweet Spirits of Nitre, Turner's Cerate. To which should be added: Common Adhesive Plaster, Isinglass Plaster, Lint, a pair of small Scales with Weights, an ounce and a drachm Measure-glass, a Lancet, a Probe, a pair of Forceps, and some curved Needles.

Many of these medicines contain lead, mercury and antimony, all of which are highly toxic. As for the forceps and needles, the average housewife was equipping herself with the means to haul a baby into the world, and to stitch up a wound, should the occasion demand. It's an approach more robust than that

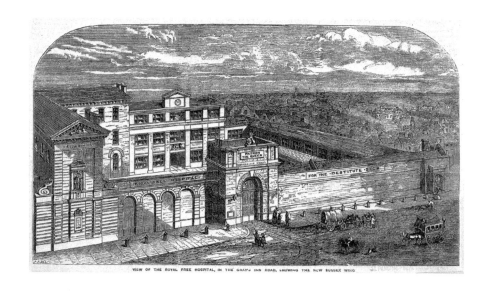

An illustration of the new Sussex Wing of The Royal Free Hospital, then in London's Gray's Inn Road, from around 1886 reinforces that it is 'For The Destitute Sick'.

of the shrinking violet more commonly associated with Victorian womanhood. And it's an approach that was cultivated out of necessity. Even amongst what we would now call healthcare professionals, there was still very little real understanding of the cause of illness and disease – and only a rather hazy understanding of anatomy. Healthcare was a private business, a commercial enterprise like any other and it operated much as it had for centuries. (There was no National Health Service until 1948.) The only free medical care came from charity hospitals, such as the Royal Free Hospital in Hampstead and some teaching hospitals.

Friendly Societies sprang up in the late eighteenth century. Members made regular payments in return for which they received help with the cost of paying for a doctor or, indeed, for a funeral. By the end of the nineteenth century, there were more than 30,000 Friendly Societies, which offered working men and women some security in times of need and protected them from debt through illness, death or old age.

HEALTHCARE PROFESSIONALS

People wanting their teeth pulled, or to be bled, might visit a barber, or even a barber surgeon, who combined skills in hairdressing, dentistry, blood-letting and surgery. Surgeons were craftsmen, who learned their skills in long apprenticeships. It was easier to become a surgeon than a physician because a would-be surgeon needed only to raise sufficient funds for an apprenticeship. By 1800, there were 8000 members of the Royal College of Surgeons.

Physicians, on the other hand, required a university education – an expensive business, which restricted access to the profession. Theoretically they were the most knowledgeable practitioners. In an era when it was rare for the sick to attend hospital, physicians made home visits, diagnosing illness and prescribing treatments. They were not, however, permitted to act as surgeons, or to dispense drugs. Indeed, physicians were often quite ignorant of the properties of the drugs they prescribed. There were far fewer practising physicians than surgeons or apothecaries: at the start of the nineteenth century, there were just 179 licensed physicians in London; by 1847, there were 643. Each might expect to earn between £1500 and £2000 per year – £88,000–117,000 in today's money.

The Victorian apothecary was a cross between a General Practitioner and a dispensing chemist. But his shop was like nothing we would recognise. There were no tempting displays of medicines, herbs or other sundries – medicines were made to order.

First Aid Kit

Victorian first aid relied on easy-to-access ingredients and herbal cures.

———•·•———

Press an ivy leaf on a cut – the rough side cleans the wound and the smooth side helps to heal it; eat an onion (raw), if one is unfortunate enough to be stung by a wasp in the throat; a soap and sugar poultice will draw out a splinter.

Oil of Earthworms

A useful linament for muscular aches and pains.

———•·•———

Dried earth worms 7 oz
Olive oil 32 fl oz
Wine 2 fl oz

Boil together until wine has evaporated. Apply by rubbing the oil into the skin.

The business of selling medicines and drugs was not a licensed activity. Indeed, grocers prescribed medicines, booksellers sold proprietary medicines, and the mail-order business in patent pills, creams and medicines was booming.

ATTEMPTS AT REGULATION

All those involved in the dispensing of drugs – apothecaries, chemists and druggists – relied on the ever-increasing number of pharmacopoeias available to learn about the latest treatments and practices. New substances were continually being uncovered. In the early part of the nineteenth century, morphine, quinine and strychnine appeared for the first time.

One of the main sources of information for physicians and apothecaries were herbals and pharmacopeia' both offering reference sources on the medicinal properties of plants and minerals. The first *London Pharmacopoeia* was not published until 1618 when a royal proclamation instructed all apothecaries follow its guide. From 1846, all the various pharmacopoeia editions – London, Edinburgh and Dublin – were absorbed into the single authoritative voice of the *British Pharmacopoeia*. Unfortunately, there was still such ignorance of the causes of disease that many of the so-called cures were mere panaceas.

Nicholas Culpeper's books, *The English Physitian* (1652) and *The Complete Herbal* (1653) were radical in that both were published in vernacular English and were designed to be self-help books for use by the poor who could not afford medical help, though doubtless those who would benefit the most were not literate enough to do so. Nevertheless Culpeper's books are said to be the most successful non-religious text ever and have been in print continuously since the seventeenth century. They provoked fury in both physicians and apothecaries alike who saw the work as a threat to their lucrative business.

But then Culpeper was highly critical of physician's skills: 'They are bloodsuckers, true vampires, have learned little since Hippocrates; use blood-letting for ailments above the midriff and purging for those below.

They evacuate and revulse their patients until they faint. Black Hellebor, this poisonous stuff, is a favourite laxative. It is surprising that they are so popular and that some patients recover. My own poor patients would not endure this taxing and costly treatment. The victims of physicians only survive since they are from the rich and robust stock, the plethoric, red-skinned residents of Cheapside, Westminster and St James.'

☠ Stramonium ☠

The Datura stramonium *cultivated in Britain. The leaves dried, collected when the plants are in flower, and the ripe seeds.*
Medicinal Properties:
Influences especially the respiratory organs. Much used in asthma; the leaf chiefly by smoking in the form of cigarettes. The extract and the tincture made of the seeds are used in convulsive coughs as antispasmodics and as anodynes in gastrodynia and other painful affections.

Apothecaries were responsible for the supply, compounding and sale of drugs, and this was how they made their living. They could also make home visits, provide medical advice and prescribe medication, but could not charge for this service. They had established their independence from the Company of Grocers in 1617 when King James I permitted the creation of The Worshipful Society of

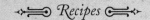

Oat Bath

To ease eczema and chickenpox sores.

———

Put two handfuls of oats into a warm bath.

Chamomile Bath

For the relief of sunburn.

———

Place a handful of dried or fresh chamomile flowers in a bag and pop in warm bath water to infuse. Leave in as you bathe.

the Art and Mystery of the Apothecaries. This established a rigorous system of apprenticeship, typically lasting seven years. If the cost of training to become a physician was prohibitive to all but a privileged few, the cost of an apprenticeship to an apothecary was still considerable; in the first half of the nineteenth century these typically were set at around 500 guineas (£28,000 in today's money). Oral examinations were conducted by members of the society to ensure the candidate was proficient in recognising ingredients as well as in the craft of handling and mixing medicines. It was only after the exam had been passed that the newly qualified apothecary could own or keep a shop. Between 1815 and 1834, six thousand new apothecaries' licences were issued, half to surgeons who were allowed to have the dual role of apothecary and surgeon.

Apothecaries did not have the social standing or wealth of the physicians, who commanded large fees from their well-to-do customers. Instead, they offered healthcare services to everyone – as was true throughout history; the first record of an apothecary's shop dates to 1345. During the Civil War (1642–49), when the rich fled the cities and were followed by their physicians, the apothecaries remained to tend to the people. Again, when the Great Plague hit London in 1665, it was the apothecaries who dared to stay. The Scottish moral philosopher Adam Smith (1723–1790) wrote in 1790 that apothecaries were 'the physicians of the poor at all times and the rich when the danger is not very great.'

From early in the eighteenth century apothecaries were legally ratified as members of the medical profession. Their role developed from dispenser of medicine, to practitioner *and* dispenser of medicine as they were allowed to prescribe medicines, a progression the physicians took great exception to. At the same time, while the apothecaries and physicians were busy defending their position in the market, new traders called chemists and druggists recognised a lucrative gap in the market and slipped in to steal a portion of the trade. This sparked the fury of both physicians and apothecaries, who accused the interlopers of muscling in on their territory, generating even more ill-feeling.

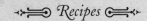

Proprietary medicines and sundries were advertised in trade periodicals to tempt the pharmacist to stock them.

Each group bickered with the other, fighting for business and professional recognition and undermining specialised professional development. Indeed, the only thing they appeared to agree about was the exclusion of women from any medical profession. However, the Apothecaries Act of 1815 gave tacit approval to the apothecary's new role of general practitioner of medicine. It also recognised

PUBLIC HEALTH

the right of chemists and druggists to prepare, compound, dispense and sell drugs and medicines.

The emergence of chemists and druggists marked the true start of the pharmacy industry. They had first appeared towards the end of the eighteenth century and spread with the increase in urbanisation offering customers a reliable outlet for the purchase of over-the-counter medicines. They stayed open for long hours and were available in emergencies, meeting the needs of a population which, far from fields, hedgerows and cottage gardens, no longer had access to the raw materials they needed for homemade remedies. Moreover, despite the furore, they were not breaking any rules, since there were no regulations for the sale of deadly poisons, such as arsenic, or addictive, over-the-counter medicines, such as laudanum, they were free to muscle in on the market. These interlopers also supplied all manner of ready-made 'proprietary' medicines: miracle cures such as Clarke's Blood Mixture, 'The World Famous Blood Purifier and Restorer'; or Burgess's Lion Ointment, 'Amputation avoided – the knife superseded.'

Chemists and druggists were not required to have dispensing qualifications. At best, they might have undertaken an apprenticeship with an apothecary, but there was no requirement for them to pass any exams. They were not permitted to prescribe as apothecaries could. Unofficially, though, they engaged in 'counter practice', recommending products for various ailments, or hurrying their customer away to seek the advice of an apothecary or physician post-haste.

A bill introduced in 1841 proposed that after 1 February 1842 no person could practice medicine without a certificate, and that after December 1842 no one could carry out the business of a chemist or druggist without a certificate. Practising medicine was defined as recommending, prescribing or ordering any medicine, remedy or application, while the chemist and druggist was defined as a person able to dispense or mix for sale any drug or medicine. However, the bill failed to get support in the House of Commons.

The group behind the bill did not give up the fight. In 1841, they proposed the formation of the Pharmaceutical Society of Great Britain (PSGB), whose function was to elevate the status of the practice of pharmacy. It aimed to head a defined and regulated programme of professional education and to unite the profession into one body. Chemists and druggists instead of being excluded, as they had always previously been, were invited to participate in the formation of the Society. Within two years, the Pharmaceutical Society had established a School of Pharmacy and had won a royal charter (1843). The title 'Royal' was granted to the society in 1988.

Legislation from 1852 established a Register of Pharmaceutical Chemists for those who had passed The Pharmaceutical Society's exams. It is at this time that the terms pharmaceutical chemist, pharmacist and pharmacy begin to enter into popular usage – the first recorded use of the word in England does not appear until the 1830s. While its use indicates the attainment of formal professional standards, the public then, as now, mixed the terms chemist, druggist and pharmacy freely to describe a shop that sold medicines.

The Medical Act of 1858 saw the faltering beginnings of a much needed process of reform; formal programmes of education were laid down to ensure that students achieved minimum standards of competence in medicine, surgery and midwifery. Regulations controlling the sale and compounding of medicines followed behind.

The Pharmacy Act of 1868 restricted the sale, dispensing and compounding of *poisons* to people who had been examined and registered by the PSGB. At this time the term 'Chemist and Druggist' was used by the PSGB to describe those who had passed its minor examination and therefore met with the minimum requirement to register as a pharmacist and the use of the title 'chemist and druggist' was restricted to legally registered pharmacists.

The formation of the Pharmaceutical Society in 1841 also saw the launch of The Pharmaceutical Journal, a monthly with a firm emphasis on pharmaceutical education and science, until 1870 when it became weekly. *The Chemist & Druggist*, a monthly trade circular, was launched in competition in 1859, it was more popularist in approach, and included regular features on the trade prices of medicinal compounds, court reports detailing many mishaps from accidentally poisoning to bankruptcy. A popular feature was the exchange of recipes.

Despite legislative controls standards were not what we might expect today. As late as 1899, Jesse Boot (1850–1931), the man who established Boots the Chemist, commented:

> *I thoroughly welcome legislation that will compel every chemist's and druggist shop, whether belonging to a company or otherwise, to be wholly and solely under the control of a registered chemist or manager. I will go further than that, and state that I should be equally glad to welcome that legislation should enforce the work of dispensing medicines should also be confined in every shop to a registered chemist.*

At the turn of the century, Jesse Boot advocated a new approach. He himself had had no prospect of becoming a qualified pharmacist since his family lacked the funds. He instigated a scheme to recruit and support promising boys through an apprenticeship, and paid them 10 shillings (10/–) weekly in the first year of apprenticeship, 12 shillings and sixpence (12/6) in the second, 15/– in the third, and 17/6 in the fourth. Assistants who had worked for Boot for more than two years were eligible to compete for four scholarships offered annually, to enable them to take a six-month full-time course at a recognised school of pharmacy and to sit the Minor examination. Jesse Boot commented:

> *Formerly the drug trade was one that could only be entered into by those having money and friends. With us a good salary is given during apprenticeship, scholarships are offered to our assistants, and after passing their examinations good and improving situations are found for them. To me the most satisfactory feature of our business is that we have men on the staff who have passed their qualifying examination with credit, and for this not to have cost their parents or friends a penny.*

Boot also encouraged chemists to give young assistants a lesson in Latin before they started work at 8 a.m. and provided training for dispensing assistants.

In the 64-year reign of Queen Victoria (1837–1901), there were revolutionary breakthroughs in the understanding and treatment of many life-threatening diseases, as well as in education and laws relating to healthcare and the provision of medicines and poisons. Consumer medicine reached the high street, creating a new medical industry that sold traditional herbal remedies as well as the newest proprietary medicines and which played a role in transforming public health. Sir Joseph Swan (1828–1914), physicist, chemist and inventor of the incandescent electric light bulb, maintained that an educated pharmacist was 'one of society's most useful and necessary members.'

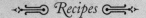

Recipes

Curry Powder

A combination of spices for cooking.

Black pepper ½ oz
Allspice ½ oz
Mustard (scorched) 1 oz
Ginger 1 oz
Fenugreek seeds 2 oz
Cinnamon bark 2 oz
Turmeric 4 oz
Coriander seeds 4 oz

Reduce all to a fine powder and mix thoroughly passing through a sieve.

Pure Liquid
Paraffin
(Paraffinum Liquidum.
A bland, odourless, tasteless oil of exceptional purity.
Specially prepared for Internal purposes.
WARNER & SON.
CHAPEL ASH.
PURE GLYCERINE
DISPENSING CHEMIST
BRIDGNORTH
MAW'S

CHAPTER 2

MEDICINE AND DISEASE

'The doctor of the future will give no medicine but will interest his patients in the care of the human frame, in diet and in the cause and prevention of disease.'

THOMAS EDISON

*I*n understanding the workings of the Victorian pharmacy, it must be acknowledged that the practice of medicine at the start of Victoria's reign had remained unchanged for many thousands of years. Statistics on life expectancy are revealing: Neolithic man had an average life span of 20 years; in the Middle Ages, the average Briton could hope to reach 30; by the end of the Victorian era, the life expectancy at birth for males was 45 years and 49 years for females. But in Victorian Britain, there was also a vast difference in the life expectancy between the poor labouring classes and the middle or upper classes; life expectancy in London in 1841 was just 37 years, dropping to 26 years of age if you lived in Liverpool. The average age of death of servants and labourers was a cautionary 16 years according to the Registrar General in 1841. By contrast, at the start of the second millennium, life expectancy for males is 76 years and 81 years for females.

At the end of the nineteenth century, figures for infant mortality were still shockingly high; it was common for 20 per cent of infants to die in their first year, in some parts that figure rose to 50 per cent. Children aged from 0-5 years of age accounted for one-third of all deaths in Victorian Britain. The tragedies that are a classic feature of our nineteenth century literary favourites formed part of the terrible reality of life. Small children were carried off with horrible monotony, fragile young men and women wasted away, and mothers and fathers were regularly felled by sudden illnesses, leaving their families destitute.

Here I am after a course of MERCURY, my teeth and gums rather the worse for it; my hair all gone, and my breath having become most intolerably offensive.

An illustration from circa 1850 shows a patient suffering from the adverse effects of mercury treatment, a medicine that was commonly prescribed to treat syphilis.

Emily Brontë's *Wuthering Heights* is littered with corpses – indeed only two servants make the transition from the beginning, to the end of the tale. Most of Dickens' heroes seem to have lost one or both parents to illness; Oliver in *Oliver Twist*, David, or Trot, in *David Copperfield*, Pip in *Great Expectations* and Little Nell in *The Old Curiosity Shop*, who proceeds to die tragically young herself. While it must be admitted that disease and death are both useful plot devices for authors, in truth they were only reflecting the harsh reality of daily life. Diseases that had plagued man for thousands of years continued to ravage populations; it seemed that the practice of medicine had not made even an iota of progress.

THE IMPACT OF FARMING

In rural areas in the Victorian era, the population was still suffering the effects of man's first move from hunter-gathering to farming. The advantage of farming was that it allowed humans to produce and store more food, enabling families to grow and groups to settle in communities. The downside was that many diseases, once exclusive to specific animal groups, now transferred to humans, a process known as zoonosis. Cattle passed on smallpox and tuberculosis; poultry and pigs passed on influenza and chickenpox; horses passed on the common cold; and measles arrived via canine distemper. In fact, humans are now believed to have more than 60 diseases in common with dogs.

Such problems still manifest themselves today; the Sars (Sudden Acute Respiratory Syndrome) virus, which spread across the world from China in 2002, was later discovered to be a corona virus that had crossed to humans from the palm civet, a cat-sized mammal sold in local markets in Guangdong. Its spread across continents was described by the World Health Organisation as a 'worldwide health threat'.

Animal husbandry is a messy business. Water polluted with human and animal faeces can spread diseases such as cholera, typhoid, polio and whooping cough. Waterholes and drainage ditches provided breeding places for mosquitoes. Food and grain attract vermin, whose fleas, the source of bubonic plague (the Black Death), travel with them and while Britain suffered no outbreaks of plague as late as the nineteenth century, it still stalked the Islamic world and China well into the nineteenth century. The possibility of it spreading across Europe, which it had done for the first time in the fourteenth century killing one-third of the population between 1347 and 1352, was a haunting spectre.

Nineteenth-century Britain may have been plague free, but nevertheless a tsunami of epidemics and infections swept across the island – in cities deaths were occurring on a scale not seen since the Black Death. Between 1831 and 1833 there were two influenza epidemics and Asiatic cholera made its first destructive appearance. Between 1836 and 1842, there were epidemics of typhus, typhoid, influenza and cholera. Incredible as it may seem, malaria was also problematic. Tuberculosis was the principle killer; it is estimated to have accounted for 20 million lives over the course of the nineteenth century.

Putting romantic notions of country life aside, the rural poor suffered from squalid living conditions. In Edwin Chadwick's report *The Sanitary Conditions of the Labouring Population* of 1842, Mr Thomas H. Smith, the medical officer of the Bromley union, describes living conditions thus:

> My attention was first directed to the sources of malaria in this district and neighbourhood when cholera became epidemic. I then partially inspected the dwellings of the poor, and have recently completed the survey. It is almost incredible that so many sources of malaria

Recipes

Insect Preventative

This recipe works admirably to repel flies, gnats and other insects.

Orris root in fine powder 20 parts
Powdered starch 75 parts
Eucalyptol 5 parts

Mix well and pass through a sieve. Apply to the skin with a powder puff.

FATHER THAMES INTRODUCING HIS O

DIPHTI

SCROFULA.   CHOLERA.

PRING TO THE FAIR CITY OF LONDON.

should exist in a rural district. A total absence of all provision for effectual drainage around cottages is the most prominent source of malaria; throughout the whole district there is scarcely an attempt at it. The refuse, vegetable and animal matters, are also thrown by the cottagers in heaps near their dwellings to decompose; are sometimes not removed, except at very long intervals; and are always permitted to remain sufficiently long to accumulate in some quantity. Pigsties are generally near the dwellings, and are always surrounded by decomposing matters. These constitute some of the many sources of malaria, and peculiarly deserve attention as being easily remedied, and yet, as it were, cherished. The effects of malaria are strikingly exemplified in parts of this district.

Nevertheless, the problem was worst in the urban areas for not only did the population suffer from the parasites and viruses passed on from animals and from those engendered by poor sanitation and hygiene, but also from overcrowded living conditions. To make matters worse, certainly in the first half of the nineteenth century, the Victorians had little understanding of the cause and effect of many diseases. Sickness was commonly attributed to bad air and bad smells and, with no attempt to rectify the root causes, epidemics spread exterminating great swathes of the populous.

SMALLPOX

Smallpox was the worst epidemic disease of the eighteenth century killing some 400,000 Europeans per year. It moved freely between rich and poor alike without respect for social barriers, it was endemic in the nineteenth century and persisted well into the early twentieth century, despite the fact that Edward Jenner (1749–1823) first demonstrated the effectiveness of cowpox vaccinations as a means of producing immunity from smallpox in 1796.

The Hampstead Smallpox Hospital was built in 1871 to meet the demands created by a continuing smallpox epidemic. The large windows offered plenty of ventilation – a Victorian obsession.

Smallpox flourished in the crowded and confined urban conurbations where large numbers of people had not yet been exposed to the disease. The *variola* virus, which causes smallpox, first makes its presence felt with 'flu-like symptoms, followed by a rash, high fever and fluid-filled blisters. Sufferers were difficult patients, becoming delirious, angry and often violent. Survivors were horribly scarred and many were left blind, indeed smallpox was said to be responsible for one-third of all cases of blindness in the seventeenth and eighteenth centuries.

The virus is spread by airborne droplets, 30 per cent of cases were fatal; infants were especially susceptible with 80 per cent of infected children dying.

The eighteenth-century mathematician and scientist the Comte de la Condamine observed, '…no man dared to count his children as his own until they had had the disease.' Esther Summerson, the kind-hearted heroine of Charles Dickens' *Bleak House*, falls prey to smallpox:

> *Dare I hint at that worse time when, strung together somewhere in great black space, there was a flaming necklace, or ring, or starry circle of some kind, of which I was one of the beads! And when my only prayer was to be taken off from the rest, and when it was such inexplicable agony and misery to be a part of the dreadful thing?*

In Edwin Chadwick's Report on *The Sanitary Condition of the Labouring Population of Great Britain*, a Dr Handley reported his experience:

> *When the small-pox was prevalent in this district, I attended a man, woman and five children, all lying in one bed-room, and having only two beds amongst them. The walls of the cottage were black, the sheets were black, and the patients themselves were blacker still; two of the children were absolutely sticking together…The smell on entering the apartments was extremely nauseous, and the room would not admit free ventilation.*

The Victorians tried to grapple with the problem mid-century with an Act of Parliament in 1853 that laid down an enforced programme of compulsory vaccination. This was the first time that the government had ever attempted to force a medical treatment on an entire population, and it met with resistance, but it was only through vaccination that the spread of the disease could be halted. Despite compulsory vaccination programmes, in Britain and across the world, it still took over a century to defeat smallpox; the World Health Organization (WHO) announced that the virus had been eradicated in 1979.

The problem was that the virus was endemic in most western countries and regular epidemics occurred. In London an epidemic between 1837 and 1840 killed 6,400 people. A particularly virulent outbreak spread across Europe

TRIUMPH OF DE-JENNER-ATION.

[The Bill for the encouragement of Small Pox awaits Third Reading in the Commons.]

1898.

Smallpox vaccination was made compulsory in 1853 but an average of 2000 people per year were prosecuted and gaoled, some repeatedly, for resisting. The Act of 1898 was amended to include a conscientious exemption clause.

In 1821 a committee of the Seamen's Hospital Society agreed to establish a floating hospital by public voluntary subscription for the relief of sick and helpless seamen, an idea that was later utilised to deal with smallpox epidemics.

between 1870 and 1875 and between the years 1871–2 alone it killed more than 50,000 people in Britain and Ireland.

In 1881, the year of the last great epidemic of smallpox in Britain, elderly warships were pressed into action to isolate the sick and to serve as floating hospitals. These were moored off Deptford Creek in south London, but when the epidemic was over the boats were moored 17 miles (27 kilometres) down river from London Bridge where they remained there until 1902, with steamers carrying patients and food out to the ships. Between the years

1884 and 1902 everyone suffering from smallpox in London was sent out to hospital ships and in that time some 20,000 people were cared for with 4000 deaths.

There was no effective treatment for smallpox; the symptoms were managed with supportive nursing. Nevertheless one so-called natural Victorian cure required the patient to mix an ounce of cream of tartar with a pint of hot water and drink when cold, a recipe that claimed to cure even the worst cases in three days. The virus now exists in just two secure laboratories in America and Russia, apparently preserved for use as a potential means of biological warfare.

SYPHILIS

Nineteenth-century London was unflatteringly known by some as 'The whore shop of the world'. By the 1850s half of the outpatients of the main London hospitals were suffering from sexually transmitted diseases (STDs), principally syphilis. Cities were estimated to have one prostitute per 12 adult males, but the problem was not restricted to Britain; physicians estimated that 15 per cent of Europe's population was infected with the disease. The problem was so great that in 1864 the British parliament passed the Contagious Diseases Act which attempted to regulate prostitution in garrison towns and ports. Its approach was brutal; a woman found within a defined radius of a garrison could be arrested and forcibly examined to determine whether or not she was suffering from an STD. Those who

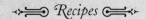

Recipes

Bergamot Tea

The tea relieves nausea and works as a mild soporific.

Fresh bergamot leaves ½ oz

Bring one pint of water to the boil then pour over the leaves and infuse for five minutes. Strain the liquid and discard leaves before drinking. Drink as required.

had contracted diseases were despatched to asylums known as 'lock hospitals' and detained for three months to keep them away from the general public. Needless to say no such treatment was handed out to men. The act was repealed in 1866.

The opening salvo of this sexually transmitted disease is genital sores followed by rashes and abscesses which eat into the bones, disfigure the face and, after long years of suffering, may lead to madness and death. It can be passed on to children in vitro, when it is known as congenital syphilis. Abraham Lincoln (1809–1865), Baudelaire (1821–1867), Van Gogh (1853–1890), Tolstoy (1828–1920) and Oscar Wilde (1854–1900), (as well as Columbus, Beethoven, Ivan the Terrible and Adolf Hitler) are all said to have suffered from it.

Treatments for syphilis commonly included ingesting mercury. The side effects were vile: excessive drooling, in the region of 1.8–2.7kg (4–6lb) of saliva a day, teeth falling out and health impairments that were often permanent. The French writer Guy de Maupassant (1850–1893) wrote of his experience of the illness in March 1887:

> *For five weeks I have been taking four centigrammes of mercury and 35 centigrammes of potassium iodide a day and I feel very well on it. Soon mercury will be my staple diet. My hair is beginning to grow again and the hair on my arse is sprouting. I've got the pox! At last! Not the contemptible clap, not the ecclesiastical crystalline, not the bourgeois coxcomb or the leguminous cauliflowers. No – no – the great pox, the one Frances I died of. The majestic pox ... and I'm proud of it, by thunder. I don't have to worry about catching it any more, and I screw the street whores and trollops, and afterwards I say to them, 'I've got the pox.' They look afraid and I just laugh.*

It is perhaps worth noting that de Maupassant spent his last days in an asylum believing that he was the wealthy younger son of the Virgin Mary and that his urine was full of jewels.

Du Maupassant's boastful and repugnant ramblings aside, the great pox was deemed to be a shameful disease. Married men who were stricken with it were reputed to give their wives chocolates laced with mercury to avoid having to confess that they had acquired the disease. American researchers finally discovered that penicillin provided an effective cure in 1943.

☠ *Gargyle, Anti-syphilitic* ☠

Take of–
Corrosive sublimate 1 grn
Extract of opium 3 grns.
Milk 1½ oz
Mucilage 6 drms.
Clarified honey 1oz
Decoction of barley 8oz

Mix

TYPHUS

Like syphilis, typhus has traditionally been regarded as a disease of war; when Napoleon invaded Russia in 1812, his troops were struck by a typhus epidemic in Moscow. More men from his 600,000-strong army were killed by typhus than by the Russians. The fever was associated with the Industrial Revolution but saw a dramatic upturn in the nineteenth century; primarily caused by the filthy living conditions of the poor in the rapidly expanding cities. Edwin

Chadwick's report *The Sanitary Conditions of the Labouring Population* of 1842 reveals that, next to consumption, fevers (typhus and scarlatina) were the biggest killers, accounting for 24,577 deaths in England and Wales in 1838 and 25,991 in 1839.

Like bubonic plague, typhus is spread by lice-infested rodents, or by human lice. Caused by the bacteria *Ricketsia prowazekii*, it causes headaches, muscle pain, fever and delirium, a rash of red spots and ultimately bleeding into the skin and swelling of the heart and the brain. Mortality rates are estimated to be between 10 and 15 per cent, though it can reach 50-60 per cent. While doctors had no cures, patented brands such as Fennings' Stomachic Mixture were produced to 'treat' fevers and flu. Later analysis of the product showed that it contained nitric acid, flavoured with peppermint and miniscule traces of organic matter including a very small amount of opium. Experts described the assertion that Fennings' Fever Curer had, for nearly 50 years, cured thousands of diseases that no other medicine could cure as a 'barefaced falsehood'.

There was a major epidemic in Ireland between 1816 and 1819, leading to an estimated 109,000 deaths, and a further outbreak during the Great Irish Famine of 1846–49. Irish emigrants fleeing the famine carried the disease to Britain and America, where it was commonly referred to as 'Irish Fever'. In Edwin Chadwick's Report Doctors Howard and Duncan relate experiences from Liverpool and Manchester:

> *In the year 1836-7, I attended a family of 13, twelve of whom had typhus fever, without a bed in the* cellar, *without straw or timber shavings-frequent substitutes. They lay on the floor, and so crowded, that I could scarcely pass between them. In another house I attended 14 patients; there were only two beds in the house. All the patients, as lodgers, lay on the boards, and during their illness, never had their clothes off.*

In Charlotte Brontë's *Jane Eyre*, the young Jane witnesses a typhus epidemic at her school:

That forest-dell, where Lowood lay, was the cradle of fog and fog bred pestilence; which, quickening with the quickening spring, crept into the Orphan Asylum, breathed typhus through its crowded schoolroom and dormitory, and, ere May arrived, transformed the seminary into a hospital.

A number of students, including Jane's close friend Helen Burns, died.

TYPHOID

Not to be confused with typhus – though the distinction was not made until the 1830s – typhoid fever is a potentially fatal bacterial infection that causes fever, flat, rose-coloured spots, abdominal pain and constipation and can lead to internal bleeding. The course of the illness lasts around four weeks and 10 per cent of infected patients could expect to die. Children and young adults were particularly susceptible. It is contracted by eating food or drinking water that has been contaminated by the *Salmonella typhi* bacteria. The resistance to the theory that polluted water might be the source of infection accounted for the continuing prevalence of typhoid, as well as other waterborne diseases, well into the nineteenth century. Even today the main protection against typhoid is a supply of pure, clean drinking water and strict food hygiene regulations.

Prince Albert, Queen Victoria's beloved husband, had a suspected attack of influenza in November 1861, but it proved to be typhoid fever and

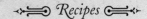

Recipes

Tarragon Digestive

Take a small measure after the evening meal as an aid to digestion.

40% or 50% Alcohol (such as vodka) 1½ pints

Fresh tarragon leaves 1 oz

Vanilla pod 1

Golden granulated sugar 12 oz

Pour the alcohol into a bottle, add the remaining ingredients. Seal and leave to infuse for month, shaking occasionally. Strain the liquid; discard the tarragon and the vanilla. Take as required.

he died on the 14th December. Ten years later the typhoid epidemic of 1870–71 afflicted the royal family again, Prince Albert Edward, later King Edward, was taken ill, but survived the fever.

Treatments up until the mid-nineteenth century revolved around purging and bleeding, but after this time doctors attempted to manage the fever with the limited means at their disposal. Home guides recommended calling in a doctor for cases of typhoid, while simultaneously recommending domestic treatment in the way of nutritious beef tea (*see right*). As with most cases of fever the wealthy were nursed at home, the poor might be despatched to a fever hospital, though fees were still payable and the very poorest might not obtain the necessary relief. The London Fever Hospital was built in Islington, to much local protest. Patients were admitted by parish order at a cost of one shilling a day, but the one hospital could not cope with the demand, more hospitals were built, but still demand could not be met and by 1881, with fever and smallpox epidemics raging, tents were erected for convalescent patients at Darenth in Kent and hospital ships were pressed into action. The workhouse infirmaries were the last hope for the desperate.

It was not until the early twentieth century that the mechanism of disease transmission was understood. In 1906, Mary Mallon, later to be nicknamed Typhoid Mary, had the singular misfortune to be the first person identified as a healthy carrier of typhoid fever. She was not alone in being a healthy carrier, but suffered for being the first to have been identified. Mary worked as a cook in America, and in 1906 six of the 11 people in her household were struck down by the fever. George Soper, an engineer with experience in typhoid fever outbreaks, was called in to establish the cause. He found out that between 1900 and 1907 Mary had held seven jobs, and in these households 22 people had become ill with typhoid. While he was investigating, Mary left her post, but Soper was able to track her down. Mary insisted she was healthy and that she could not have been the carrier. She stoutly refused to supply a stool and blood sample and fought impressively to maintain her innocence.

Dr Sara Josephine Baker was despatched to persuade her to provide the necessary samples:

She came out fighting and swearing, both of which she could do with appalling efficiency and vigor. I made another effort to talk to her sensibly and asked her again to let me have the specimens, but it was of no use. By that time she was convinced that the law was wantonly persecuting her, when she had done nothing wrong. She knew she had never had typhoid fever; she was maniacal in her integrity. There was nothing I could do but take her with us. The policemen lifted her into the ambulance and I literally sat on her all the way to hospital; it was like being in a cage with an angry lion.

Mary was twice quarantined against her wishes on North Brother Island. The first time was for three years, after which she was released if she agreed to stop working as a cook. Unfortunately, she returned to her original profession. She was tracked down five years later after more deaths occurred, and was incarcerated until her death 23 years later. She is thought to have infected 47 people, causing three deaths.

A human carrier is a healthy person who has survived an episode of typhoid, but in whom the typhoid bacteria survive without causing any further symptoms. The bacteria are excreted in faeces and urine, and it takes careful scrubbing with soap and hot water to remove the bacteria from the hands. Mary was unique in that she was the only carrier who refused to accept her status and who knowingly went back to working in kitchens, despite

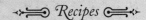
Beef Tea

A favourite to fend off the winter chills.

1 lb of beef free from fat to be minced very small, mixed with an equal weight of cold water and heated slowly to boiling. When it has boiled for a minute or two, strain through a cloth. It may be coloured with roasted onion or burnt sugar and salted to the taste.

her promise not to do so. It is thought that Mary was borne a carrier because her mother had typhoid fever during her pregnancy. In Britain carriers could be locked up in asylums. Figures from Long Grove Asylum in Epsom, Surrey, show 43 healthy female typhoid carriers were locked up for life between 1907 and its closure in 1992. The last major outbreak in Britain was in 1964 when a contaminated can of corned beef from Argentina spread the infection to other produce in the supermarket after it was opened and sold sliced, 500 people were hospitalised.

DIPHTHERIA

Diphtheria is a highly contagious and life-threatening infection that attacks the membranes of the throat and nose. A tough membrane forms, which causes bronchial obstruction and suffocation; small children are particularly susceptible. In his book *The Horse and Buggy Doctor*, Arthur Hertzler (1870–1946) recalled standing at a window as a small child and watching a line of wagons travelling down the road. Each wagon contained a small wooden box, and as the days went on he learned that the boxes contained the bodies of many of his friends:

> *Eight of the nine children in that one family died of diphtheria in ten days. There remained only a baby of nine months. The mother took to carrying this child constantly, even when she did the farm housework. Clutched to her mother's breast, this child seemed inordinately wide-eyed, as though affected by the silent grief that surrounded her.*

In New York in 1880, 4000 cases of diphtheria were reported, and of these 50 per cent were fatal. The disease crossed all social barriers, affecting rich and poor alike: Princess Alice, Queen Victoria's third child, nursed five of her children with diphtheria, her youngest, Princess May, died aged four and eventually Alice herself also succumbed to the disease dying a month later in December 1878 aged 35.

Again there was no cure, those recovering might be given tonics to help build up their strength. Vibrona Tonic Wine, which had a royal warrant, and was recommended for those recuperating from diphtheria, contained alcohol and sugar as well as cinchona – quinine. The German physiologist Emil von Behring discovered the diphtheria antitoxin in 1890, and was awarded a Nobel Prize for his work in 1901. However the vaccine was not used in a national programme until the 1920s – it is part of the childhood immunisation programme today and cases of diphtheria still occur.

CHOLERA

In the nineteenth century, *Cholera asiatica* quickly established itself as a deadly disease. It was endemic in the Indian subcontinent, but in the early nineteenth century it became pandemic, spreading to Egypt, North Africa and Russia, and then, in the summer of 1831, across Europe. The first outbreak in Britain was in Sunderland on the Durham coast in autumn 1831. It spread north to Scotland and south to London, accounting for 7000 deaths in London alone in 1832, overall the outbreak claimed 52,000 lives. In a span of 14 years in Russia, it killed over a million people, including the composer Tchaikovsky (1840–1893). Britain experienced four major cholera epidemics in the nineteenth century which are said to have accounted for 140,000 deaths. At such times churchyards were closed when full and the dead were buried in unconsecrated ground.

Outbreaks of cholera caused public panic, affected areas were quarantined and relief *might* be made available in the way of food distribution. The Liverpool Chronicle of the 2nd June 1982 reports the following public response to an outbreak:

> *Stones and brickbat were thrown at the premises, several windows were broken, even in the room where the woman, now in a dying state, was lying, and the medical gentleman who was attending her was obliged to seek safety in flight. Several individuals were pursued and attacked by the mob and some hurt. The park constables were apparently panic struck, and incapable of acting....*

BOARD OF WORKS
FOR THE LIMEHOUSE DISTRICT.
COMPRISING LIMEHOUSE, RATCLIFF, SHADWELL & WAPPING.

In consequence of the appearance of **CHOLERA** within this District, the Board have appointed the under-mentioned Medical Gentlemen who will give ADVICE, MEDICINE, AND ASSISTANCE, FREE OF ANY CHARGE, AND UPON APPLICATION, AT ANY HOUR OF THE DAY OR NIGHT.

The Inhabitants are earnestly requested not to neglect the first symptoms of the appearance of Disease, (which in its early stage is easy to cure), but to apply, WITHOUT DELAY, to one of the Medical Gentlemen appointed.

The Board have opened an Establishment for the reception of Patients, in a building at Green Bank, near Wapping Church, (formerly used as Wapping Workhouse), where all cases of Cholera and Diarrhœa will be received and placed under the care of a competent Resident Medical Practitioner, and proper Attendants.

THE FOLLOWING ARE THE MEDICAL GENTLEMEN TO BE APPLIED TO:--

Mr. ORTON,
56, White Horse Street.

Dr. NIGHTINGALL,
4, Commercial Terrace, Commercial Road, (near Limehouse Church.)

Mr. SCHROEDER,
53, Three Colt Street, Limehouse.

Mr. HARRIS,
5, York Terrace, Commercial Road, (opposite Stepney Railway Station.)

Mr. CAMBELL,
At Mr. GRAY's, Chemist, Old Road, opposite "The World's End."

Mr. LYNCH,
St. James's Terrace, Back Road, Shadwell.

Mr. HECKFORD,
At the Dispensary, Wapping Workhouse.

By Order,

BOARD OFFICES, WHITE HORSE STREET,
26th July, 1866.

THOS. W. RATCLIFF,
Clerk to the Board.

Cholera is caused by poor sanitation and is highly infectious. Vomiting and extreme diarrhoea quickly send the body into shock, dehydration rapidly occurs and death can follow, all within 18 hours. Towards the end, the dehydrated patient has a hollowed face and blue lips. The Victorians believed that it was caused by rancid or putrid food, by 'cold food' such as melon and cucumber, and by passionate fear or rage. In fact, the term cholera was often used to describe any acute attack of diarrhoea – a point worth remembering given that one-quarter of all deaths in children under five was attributed to childhood diarrhoea. A cholera epidemic in Liverpool in 1849 claimed 5,308 lives and, in the same year, 1,834 lives were lost in Hull.

In 1854 a London epidemic accounted for 10,738 lives, one outbreak in central London had killed 700 people in under two weeks before it was famously halted by the physician John Snow. He undertook a painstaking investigation, talking to local residents and plotting the cases of cholera on a map of the area:

> *On proceeding to the spot, I found that nearly all the deaths had taken place within a short distance of the [Broad Street] pump. There were only ten deaths in houses situated decidedly nearer to another street-pump.*

Asiatic cholera appeared in Britain for the first time in 1831. Devastating epidemics rampaged through the country killing thousands and causing widespread panic; posters were used to relay essential health information.

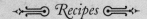

Chervil Water

A gentle cleanser for delicate skins.

Take a handful of chervil leaves and infuse in water that has been boiled for 10 minutes.

Chamomile Rinse

Use as a rinse to brighten and lighten blonde hair.

Handful of dried or fresh chamomile flowers

Put a couple of pints of water on to boil. Remove from the heat, add the flowers and leave to infuse for five minutes. Strain the liquid then use as a rinse as required.

In five of these cases the families of the deceased persons informed me that they always sent to the pump in Broad Street, as they preferred the water to that of the pumps which were nearer. In three other cases, the deceased were children who went to school near the pump in Broad Street... With regard to the deaths occurring in the locality belonging to the pump, there were 61 instances in which I was informed that the deceased persons used to drink the pump water from Broad Street, either constantly or occasionally... The result of the inquiry, then, is, that there has been no particular outbreak or prevalence of cholera in this part of London except among the persons who were in the habit of drinking the water of the above-mentioned pump well.......

I had an interview with the Board of Guardians of St James's parish, on the evening of the 7th inst [Sept 7], and represented the above circumstances to them. In consequence of what I said, the handle of the pump was removed on the following day.'

John Snow, letter to the editor of the Medical Times and Gazette *23rd September 1854.*

It was discovered later that this public water supply was sited only 3ft (90cm) from a cesspit, which was leaking faecal matter. An epidemic in the East End of London in 1866 took 5,596 lives just when work on London's sewage system was nearly completed.

The appalling housing conditions and sanitation of early Victorian Britain were the perfect breeding ground for the disease. In Edwin Chadwick's report of 1842 a Mr Baker reports on the sanitary conditions found in Leeds:

In one cul-de-sac, *in the town of Leeds, there are 34 houses, and in ordinary times, there dwell in these houses 340 persons, or ten to every house; but as these houses are many of them receiving houses for itinerant labourers, during the periods of hay-time and harvest and the fairs, at least twice that number are then here congregated. The name of this place*

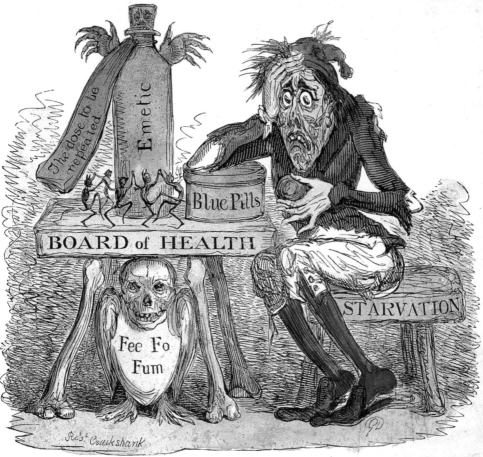

ROBERT CRUIKSHANK'S

RANDOM SHOTS.—(N.º 2.)

The dose to be repeated

Emetic

Blue Pills

BOARD of HEALTH

Fee Fo Fum

STARVATION

Rob.ª Cruikshank

Published by TOMLINSON,   24, Great Newport Street.

A CHOLERA PATIENT.

A caricature from 1832 shows a cholera sufferer experimenting with remedies. There were no cures for cholera, though this didn't stop physicians and pharmacists from proffering weird and wonderful treatments such as blue pills, which contained mercury.

is the Boot and Shoe-yard, in Kirkgate, a location from' whence the Commissioners removed, in the days of the cholera, 75 cart-loads of manure, which had been untouched for years, and where there now exists a surface of human excrement of very considerable extent, to which these'; impure and unventilated dwellings are additionally exposed. This property is said to pay the best annual interest of any cottage property in the borough.

The same report contains an account of the typical living conditions of a cholera patient from a Mr. James Bland, medical officer of the Macclesfield union:

I beg to observe that the lodging-houses are a fruitful source of fever. The persons renting these tenements showed greater resistance than others in having their houses properly whitewashed at the time the epidemic cholera appeared. The vagrants who visit these houses are frequently attacked with fever: exposed during the day to the inclemency of the seasons, with their imperfect covering, ragged clothes, and naked feet, at night thrust into a room perhaps of 16 or 20 square yards, having perhaps five or six beds and three individuals in a bed, married and single, male and female, to all appearance indiscriminately lodged. When a case of illness occurs, the lodging-house keeper is most importunate and clamorous in demanding relief from the town; and when obtained, it is quite a question whether it will really be applied to the wants of the sufferer. I have never any confidence that the remedies given will be administered to the patient.

The great German physician Robert Koch (1843–1910), who is considered one of the fathers of microbiology, isolated the *Vibrio cholera* bacteria in 1884. By this point, however, improved public health measures were already beginning to have an impact on the number of cholera outbreaks.

Nevertheless, throughout most of the century, the cause of cholera was unknown and there were no effective treatments save hydration and management. Copies of the Lancet, from 1849, detail some case studies titled as follows: 'Treatment of Cholera by Small and Repeated Doses of Calomel'; 'Report of a Case of Cholera Treated by Transfusion'; 'On the Employment of Embrocations and Injections of Strong Liquid Ammonia in the Collapse Stage of Cholera.' Like as not the doctor might recommend cholera drops – a liquid mix often containing opium and menthol, camphor and chloroform, or a cholera mixture which contained most of the above, plus creosote!

TUBERCULOSIS

Tuberculosis (TB), also known as phthisis, was one of the great scourges of Victorian Britain and said to account for between 60,000 and 70,000 deaths in each decade of Victoria's reign. It is estimated to have been the single biggest killer in the mid-nineteenth century. It was also known as galloping consumption, because people suffering from it seemed to be consumed at speed from within. It is caused by *Mycobacterium tuberculosis*, which affects the lungs and is an airborne disease spread by spit, sneezes and coughs and is, therefore contagious. The symptoms are a chronic cough, blood-tinged sputum, fever, night sweats and weight loss. The infection can be permanently arrested, but it can also break out again when the immune system is depleted. If allowed to progress it destroys large areas of the lungs.

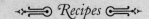

Recipes

Rosemary Water

Soothes external aches and pains.

Fresh rosemary flowering tips
4 tablespoons
Ethyl alcohol ¼ pint

Put the ingredients into an airtight jar and leave in a cool dark place for two weeks, shake the jar occasionally. Strain the liquid into a clean bottle and store.

TB was not recognised as a disease until the 1820s. Robert Koch identified the bacteria responsible in 1882, but there was no cure. Patients were despatched to warm climates and sanatoria to rest, or they might try their luck at The Royal Seabathing Hospital at Margate, which specialised in the treatment of TB, notably scrofula, a skin disease that is caused by TB. It was not until 1946, with the development of the antibiotic streptomycin, that a cure was possible.

The Brontë family were wiped out by TB. The two eldest sisters, Maria and Elizabeth died in childhood. They had been sent to a school at Cowan's Bridge for clergyman's daughters, along with Emily and Charlotte. Their treatment was so shocking that it resulted in the deaths of the older girls and was the inspiration for Lowood School in Charlotte Brontë's *Jane Eyre*. Maria, the eldest child, was said to have inspired the character of Helen Burns, she died in 1825 aged 11. Elizabeth was to follow her six weeks later aged just 10. Branwell Brontë was the next to die on the 24th September 1848 aged 31, three months before his sister Emily, who died aged 30, on the 19th December 1848. Two weeks after Emily's death Anne fell ill from consumption, she took a trip to Scarborough with Charlotte five months later because she wanted to see the sea again. She died there four days later, on the 28th May 1849, aged 29 and is the only family member not to be buried in the family vault at St Michael and All Angels, Haworth. Charlotte, who was pregnant, died of TB at the age of 38 on 31st March 1855. All the sisters struggled bravely on to the end, Emily herself refused to see a doctor until noon on the day of her death, she died just two hours later.

The poets Shelley and Keats were sufferers, indeed, it is likely that Keats infected Shelley. Keats, who had trained as an apothecary, was bled, given opiates and deliberately starved – allowed just an anchovy and a piece of bread a day, to reduce the blood flow to his stomach. Not surprisingly, the treatment that is thought to have hastened his death, contributing as it did to his overall weakness. Sadly, Keats understood the nature of his disease from his training, and from nursing his brother Tom, who also died of the disease.

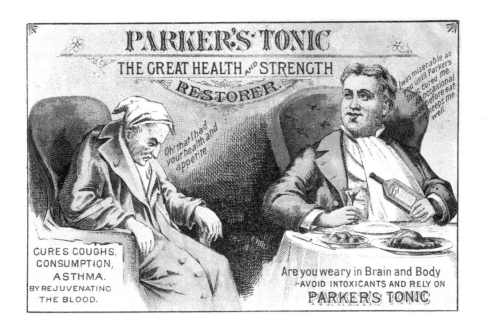

An advertisement from the 1870s bows to the temperance movement by advising the avoidance of intoxicants. Ironically, an analysis of Parker's Tonic revealed that it contained 42.6 per cent alcohol.

☠ *Popular Remedy for Consumption* ☠

Rum, half a pint
Linseed oil, honey, garlic (beaten to a pulp) and loaf sugar, of each 4oz.
Yolks of five eggs, mix.
A teaspoonful night and morning

The poet's first lung haemorrhage, on 3 February 1820, one year after the birth of Princess Alexandrina Victoria, was described by his close friend, Charles Brown. Keats was coming for a visit and arrived late and very cold. Brown sent him straight to bed, then took him a glass of spirits. As he entered the room, he heard Keats give a cough. It was just a slight cough, but Keats said, 'That is blood from my mouth.' There was blood on the bed sheet and he asked his friend Brown to bring a candle so that he could inspect it. He then calmly observed: 'I know the colour of that blood; it is arterial blood. I cannot be deceived in that colour. That drop of blood is my death warrant. I must die.' Keats' health deteriorated steadily after the initial haemorrhage and he passed away in Rome on 23 February 1821.

The writer Anton Chekov also died of TB, in 1908. His wife Olga described his last moments:

> *Anton sat up unusually straight and said loudly and clearly, 'I'm dying'. The doctor calmed him, took a syringe and gave him an injection of camphor, and ordered champagne. Anton took a full glass, examined it, smiled at me and said: 'It's a long time since I drank champagne.' He drained it, lay quietly on his left side, and I just had time to run to him and lean across the bed and call to him, but he had stopped breathing and was sleeping as peacefully as a child.*

Even today, with antibiotics, the disease takes a long time to clear and increasingly some strains are becoming drug resistant.

Diseases such as syphilis, cholera and TB were the day-to-day business of the pharmacist, chemist and druggist. And, as if these alone were not bad enough, then measles, scarlet fever, whooping cough, polio and influenza all required careful treatment and could kill. Even gastroenteritis or diarrhoea could be fatal and given the quality of the food and water available both regularly were.

There were eight influenza epidemics between 1830 and 1846 alone, those that survived were left weak and often unable to fight off other diseases. The influenza pandemic of 1889–92 carried off the heir to the throne, Prince Albert Victor, eldest son of Bertie, the Prince of Wales, and Princess Alexandra. He died in 1892, leaving his brother George to succeed his father in 1910.

In 1840 scarlet fever was responsible for 20,000 deaths in one year. In just two years in England and Wales, between 1838 and 1840, measles and whooping cough accounted for 50,000 deaths. In many cases the best assistance that the physician, apothecary or chemist could offer was hope and their desperate customers were quite prepared to pay for it – whatever form it took.

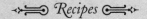

Sprain Oil

To treat the bruising and swelling caused by ligament sprains.

Take a handful and a half each of rue, red sage, lavender, rosemary, chamomile, and sweet bay and pound together in a mortar; add one-quarter of a pint of sweet almond oil; simmer it over the fire for an hour and a half; strain it through a linen cloth; add 1 oz of spike lavender, and it is fit for use.

CHAPTER 3

THE CHEMIST AND HIS SHOP

'FOR IMMEDIATE DISPOSAL: in a Sea Port Town, a Retail and Prescribing Business, established 3 years by present proprietor, who, owing to ill-health, is going further inland. Returns £285 and gradually increasing. Incoming about £150.'

THE CHEMIST & DRUGGIST 15TH JULY 1868

*M*ost chemists and druggists started as tradesmen, good businessmen who recognised the lucrative potential of the health market. Early in Victoria's reign few were qualified to dispense prescriptions; the trade was unregulated and anyone could operate under the title chemist and druggist. Legal controls were minimal until the Pharmacy Act of 1868, and were fairly ineffectual even after that. But as the training for chemists, druggists and pharmacists – the latter the newest moniker for fully trained and qualified dispensers of medicine, was regulated the business moved from that of a trade to a respected profession.

Nevertheless it was a business like any other, and throughout Victoria's reign each pharmacist had to keep a wary eye on their competitors. In *Blackwood's Magazine* in July 1841, publisher John Murray observed:

> *In nothing is the deadly struggle for existence so manifest throughout London, as in the rivalry of doctor's shops; they divide with licensed*

Pharmacists kept a ledger of every prescription they made up containing the date, the nature of the prescription, the patient's name, address and profession. ☞

victuallers all the comers; their blue and red lights stream like meteors on this
side and on that, ominously portentous; they will bleed for a penny, cup for
twopence, and draw teeth for nothing; they will give you physic enough to
poison a regiment for a groat, and offer advice at its actual value – advice
gratis. … When we use the word doctor in talking of medical establishments,
we cannot be supposed to include gentlemen regularly educated in, and
legally qualified for the profession; we animadvert [pass criticism] solely on
the swarms of chemists, who, without education, qualification, or experience,
impudently take upon themselves to prescribe for all manner of ailments.

So why were chemists so popular? The simple answer is that they allowed people to maintain control over their medication. They obligingly sold them whatever they requested, whether proprietary medicines, patent remedies or nostrums – herbal cures made specifically to old family recipes and they kept their costs down. They leapt with enthusiasm on any new product that might tickle the fancy of their customers, and supplied all the old traditional cures. By the mid-nineteenth century, in a free market, they were the main suppliers of medicines and health products.

THE PROFESSIONAL CHEMIST

Then, as now, the chemist's shop was intensely alluring, packed full of interesting smelling lotions and potions in bottles of all shapes, sizes and colours. Physicians and apothecaries were put out by the arrival of these upstarts, who frequently undercut them on costs, but the public flocked to them. A report from the Select Committee on Medical Poor Relief from 1844 claimed that the 'ignorant and uninformed' looked for aid from inferior sources:

the easy access to the druggist's shop, vying with the gin palace in its
tempting decorations, attracts those who prefer spending a few pence to
encountering the formalities and delay attendant on an application to a
qualified practitioner. Then the speedy apprehension of the case by the
druggist's shopman, a glance being sufficient to satisfy him both as to its

nature and treatment, and his ready selection
of some drug as a certain cure for the malady of
the customer, all this tells wonderfully on the
ignorant of all classes.

The report concludes with the alarming prophecy: 'The inevitable results to the community are fearful loss of life and destruction of health.'

The issue of unqualified chemists or pharmacists giving advice on health matters was a thorny one, but not as straightforward as it might appear. Jacob Bell (1810–1859), founder of The Pharmaceutical Society of Great Britain, explained that a chemist 'cannot avoid occasionally giving advice, without incurring the imputation of ignorance and losing the confidence of his customers…' It must also be acknowledged that many customers were illiterate and simply could not manage without the guidance of a chemist, being unable to afford to consult an apothecary or physician.

Early chemists were entrepreneurs, willing to try to make, or purchase, anything their customers required, and they had to be open to innovation and new developments in botany, science and technology. Many everyday products, such as matches, soap powder and table salt, were developed as a direct result of pharmacists personal experiments. Chemists also had to have a myriad of skills, including stock-taking, book-keeping, accounts and publicity. They kept a longhand record of every prescription dispensed, detailing the name, address and profession of the recipient.

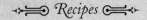

Recipes

Oatmeal Paste

A relief for sore or chapped hands.

Mix a quarter of a pound of unsalted hog's lard with a few drops of rosewater, the yolks of two new laid eggs, and a large spoonful of honey. Add as much fine oatmeal as will work into the mixture to make a thick paste.

One pharmacist, a Mr Llewellyn, kept a heart-rending scrapbook of notes passed to him from customers, which he titled *Trials of a Pharmacist*. These are shocking as much for their poor standard of literacy, which the chemist had to try to decipher, as well as for their naïve faith in the chemist's ability to resolve all manner of problems: 'Please send me some 3d pills to remove the bowels,' asks one customer. Another pleads: 'Dear Sir will you give this young man some thing for me as I want it to wich [sic] craft some one as they won't let me alone as they are down on me and I cant [sic] rest'. Most requests were written in pencil on tiny scraps of paper torn from bags: '3 Penny Mouth Dull water for eye cups for baby', which Mr Llewellyn understood to mean dill water required for hiccups. Then there was a request for '6d Fox's Lungs Syrup of Squirrels', which he took to be a request for the patent brand Fox's Lung Syrup of Squills. The squill is the bulb of the sea onion and was used as an expectorant in the treatment of asthma, bronchitis and coughs.

 *Instantaneous Toothache-cure*

Finest mastic 6 drachms
Extract of Indian Hemp 1 oz
Chloroform 1oz

Mix and shake occasionally until dissolved

Hydrochlorate of morphia 30 grains
Menthol 1 drachm
Chloral hydrate 2 drachms
Camphor 4 drachms
Oil of cajaput 2 drachms
Tincture of pellitory 4oz

Mix, and shake occasionally until dissolved, then add the mastic solution and filter.

Label Instantaneous Toothache Cure:
A few drops to be applied to cotton-wool
This is both an anodyne and a protective.
It is very efficient and becomes popular.

APPRENTICES AND ASSISTANTS

The chemist was lord and master of his domain. Indeed, he usually lived above the shop, working long hours to ensure the success of their business. Jesse Boot recalls that he worked a 16-hour day, starting at 7a.m., throughout the week:

> *Every night, after the shop closed at 9 p.m.*
> *I had to go through the stock and re-order*
> *owing to the shortage, thus working five*
> *nights a week until eleven or eleven-thirty*
> *and on Saturdays we kept open until 11pm.*

He described much of the work as being monotonous. Many products had to be made by hand: his mother prepared herbal remedies at the back, notably Boot's Lobelia Pills.

For obvious reasons, chemists depended on their apprentices and assistants. Distinguished by their long aprons, they helped with the dispensing and also kept the shop sparkling. The basic wages for a shop assistant could range from £20 per year to £50, rising with experience. Assistants were required to be literate and good at mathematics, for they had to write bills and add up totals. Good manners were important, as was a good personal appearance; they

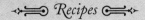

Liquid Dentifrice

To freshen the breath.

Castille soap (white) 2 oz
Distilled water 8 oz
Oil of cinnamon 10 drops
Oil of orange 10 drops
Rectified spirit (such as vodka) 8 oz
Liquid cochineal as desired

Cut the soap into fine shreds and dissolve in the water over a gentle heat. Dissolve the oils in the spirit and add to the soap solution, stirring constantly. Colour with cochineal as desired.

needed to inspire confidence in the customers. If there was space above the shop, the assistants sometimes lived there. Many chemists also employed errand boys to drop off parcels and prescriptions once they had been prepared.

The situations vacant column of *The Chemist & Druggist* reveals something of the skills required and salaries on offer. The following advertisements were placed in the issue of 15 July 1868, in the section 'Employers Seeking Assistants'. Note the emphasis on stature:

> • *Wanted an active industrious Young Man as Assistant. Must be able to extract teeth. Address stating age, height and salary.*
> • *Junior Assistant Wanted at B. Musso's English Dispensing Establishment, 6 Rue de Pont Neuf, Nice. Salary £8 per month, for journey money, £5. Address post paid, with photograph, stating age, height, references.*

The staff in chemist outlets worked long hours, six days a week, and many establishments stayed open late. Bob Elliott began as an errand boy in 1881 for Jesse Boot:

> *In anticipation of the rush on Saturdays there was a good supply of everything that could be weighed up in the quantities expected to be sold, this work occupying the spare time throughout the week and being participated in by all the counter men. There were some lines though, which were not packed more than a few hours before selling and these, when big lines, were rather a bother. Three such lines which we used to sell in enormous quantities in the hot weather were 'Boiling' Magnesia, Saline and Lemon Kali, which were located on the grocery side of the shop. 8 o'clock was the time for opening the shop and within a few minutes of that hour all the assistants had arrived. With the smallest time possible given to 'dusting' etc., the assistants on this side of the shop took off their coats and started to*

'weigh up' these articles in ¹/₄–lbs., ¹/₂–lbs., etc., working at their fastest: by about 10.15 there would be stacks of these things sufficient to last until the evening. So the day started with two hours' hard work preliminary to the rush of customers. The assistants would then put on their coats and clean white aprons, ready for the fray. By that time customers would be coming in a steady stream.

HERBALISM AND THE ORIGINS OF BOOTS THE CHEMIST

Many chemists and druggists started trading with herbal preparations, but they also developed their own preparations. When one took over the business from another he acquired the rights to all the recipes associated with the business. The trade magazine *The Chemist & Druggist*, first published in 1859; encouraged its readers to try to make new products and provided many helpful recipes, liberal individuals sent in their most efficacious recipes for publication so that others might benefit from their success.

Given that the physician's standard treatments – blood-letting, and the toxic nature of their medicines which induced purging and sweating (*see* Chapter 4: Poison) – were inevitably doomed to failure in a percentage of cases, it is no wonder that the public were so ready to use the herbal remedies that had sustained their parents and grandparents. Most families were familiar with these treatments and placed great faith in them.

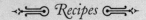

Recipes

Fennel Tea

A great aid for digestion and to relieve constipation.

Put 1 teaspoon of dried fennel seeds into a cup and pour boiling water over the top. Leave to infuse for five minutes, then strain and discard the seeds before drinking.

Peppermint Tea

Drink one to three cups as you like to relieve the pain of a headache.

Put a few leaves in boiling water and inhale to ease nasal congestion. Children may prefer spearmint tea for its milder taste

Whatever their value, even the Victorian physician was aware of the power of the placebo effect – the positive physiological reaction to any substance, no matter how inert, which the patient attributes to the medication.

In the countryside the poor had to help themselves for no one else would; there were no over-the-counter remedies for sale here, proprietary medicines were only available via mail order and an apothecary, who could dispense expensive drugs, might be many miles distant. Homemade herbal remedies were often the only medicine to be had and, blessedly, the raw ingredients were often to be had for the taking from the hedgerow. Flora Thompson's (1876–1947) semi-autobiographical account of life in the late nineteenth century, *Lark Rise'*, highlights the continued importance of the use of herbs: 'The village women cultivated a herb corner, stocked with thyme and parsley and sage for cooking, rosemary to flavour the home made lard, lavender to scent the best clothes and peppermint, pennyroyal, horehound, camomile, tansy, balm and rue for physic. They made a good deal of chamomile tea which they drank freely to ward off colds, to soothe the nerves and as a general tonic. … the women had a private use for the pennyroyal, though, judging from appearances it was not very effective.' Pennyroyal was widely regarded as an abortifactant and chemists were commonly asked for a medication 'to remove obstructions'. However, she notes that even in the rural communities the traditional herbal skills were waning: 'As well as the garden herbs, still in general use, some of the older women used wild ones, which they gathered in their seasons and dried. But the knowledge and use of these was dying out.'

☠ *British Herb Tobacco* ☠

The principle ingredient in this compound is dried coltsfoot leaves, to which a smaller portion of thyme, wood-betony, eye-bright and rosemary are added.

By now, the use of herbs had moved from traditional practice into a system that had, to an extent been standardised, receiving 'proper' recognition. Samuel

Thomson (1769–1843) was a self-taught herbalist from New Hampshire, who put his faith in herbal treatments after physicians had failed him. Thomson believed that all ill health was caused by cold and that a cure could be effected by the removal of toxins from the system – a principle not dissimilar to the orthodox medicine of the time. He therefore recommended a combination of steam baths, combined with herbs such as cayenne pepper and *Lobelia inflata* (puke weed), whose seeds induce vomiting and perspiration. After practising for 10 years, he wrote a book and sold patents to use his system of medicine, the Thomsonian System, for 20 dollars. His remedies and herbs were very popular until the middle of the nineteenth century and were particularly important to families living many miles from the nearest town and any form of medical help.

The system was brought to England by an American, Dr A. I. Coffin, who toured London and the northern industrial towns to promote the concept and selling his own publication *The Botanic Guide to Health*. John Boot (1815–1860) heard a talk by one of Dr Coffin's disciples and was immediately attracted to the Thomsonian System. A committed Methodist, he was interested in the spiritual and bodily welfare of his neighbours and had learned about herbs and herbal remedies from his mother. Boot opened a shop in Goosegate in Nottingham, in 1849, which he called the British and American Botanic Establishment. He offered consultations on Mondays, Wednesdays and Saturdays; the other days were presumably given over to collecting wild herbs from the nearby

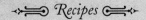

Recipes

Hair Oil

For instant shine and a glossy touch.

Nut oil 20 oz
Olive oil 40 oz
Alcohol 5 oz
Essence of musk ½ oz
Oil of bergamot ½ oz
Oil of orange 140 drops
Rose otto oil 18 drops

Place all the ingredients in a bottle and shake well.

countryside and the concoction of herbal remedies. Herbal mixtures could be purchased to deal with 'female complaints', 'chronic cough' and 'consumption'. Boot was so successful that two rival establishments set up in competition.

In an article published in a Nottingham newspaper in 1943, a man recalls his experience of visiting John Boot's shop about 1865–6:

> *It was just an ordinary herbal store with its bunches of dried herbs hanging from the top and sides of the window and small bowls and saucers containing seeds, dried roots etc, …I was employed as errand boy at the shop next door, Mr Avery Wain, brush manufacturer &c., and Mrs Boot used to borrow me from Mr Wain to run her errands and took a great interest in me. … I remember her cutting open a large poppy head. She showed me the vast number of seeds it contained, pointing out to me how very like a cod fish's roe, and explaining how great and beautiful our Great Creator is to us. I have never forgotten that lesson and I wonder if she taught the same lesson to her son, and if acting on the lines of it he produced his mammoth business out of the thoughts of those small seeds.*

JESSE BOOT

John Boot died aged 44, leaving a widow, Mary, and two children, Jesse and Jane. The shop was Mary Boot's only source of income and so she continued in the venture of medical botany, but gave up consultations. She continued collecting herbs with her children, often working barefoot because wet grass was not good for their leather boots, which were reserved for shop use and Sunday best. Both the children also learned how to dry and store herbs and how to prepare various pills and potions.

Jesse joined his mother in the shop when he was 13 years old; he took sole control at the tender age of 27. Boot realised that medical botany was not as popular as it had once been and looked for new ways to boost his business, including expanding his range on offer and selling goods at highly competitive prices. He said later:

... there was nothing at all remarkable about my methods. They were simply the application of common sense. I found that everywhere articles, especially drugs, were being sold at ridiculously high prices, and were sold without any regard to neatness and attractiveness. My idea was simply to buy tons where others bought hundredweights or less, thus buying much more cheaply, and making all the articles I sold look as attractive as possible. ... On patent medicines too, I found that I could knock off twopence or so, and still make a nice little profit.

Jesse Boot went on to transform the small herbal store into a powerful pharmaceutical giant, Boots the Chemist. In just 25 years, he increased the number of stores from 1 to 250.

THE NEW MEDICINES

Sales of proprietary medicines were, as Jesse Boot observed, an increasingly profitable part of any chemist's business. A proprietary medicine had a registered trademark, which protected the product name and allowed the manufacturer to keep his formula secret, a system that discouraged imitation and maximised the profits from advertising. Some such products contained little more than water, colouring and flavouring. Others trumpeted exotic ingredients such as snake oil, which suggested special curative properties. Many were downright dangerous: cures for colds could contain heroin or cocaine;

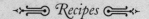

Marshmallow Lotion
An effective relief for dry hands.

Freshly grated marshmallow
(Althea officinalis) root 1 oz
Ground almonds 2 tablespoons
Milk 1 dessertspoon
Cider vinegar 1 teaspoon

Place the grated marshmallow root in a bowl and pour over ¼ pint of cold water and leave to soak for 24 hours. Strain the liquid, put 1 tablespoonful into a container, add the ground almonds, milk and cider vinegar and beat together until well mixed. This makes a runny, gritty, soothing solution, it will only keep for a few days, but the marshmallow root liquid can be stored in an airtight container and used again as required in fresh batches of mixture.

Ointment for Ringworm

A topical cream to be patted on to the skin.

———

Melt together equal parts of thymol and lard; in a hot water bath they mix perfectly.

Custard Powder

A warming accompaniment to puddings and desserts.

———

Essence of lemon 40 drops
Essence of almonds 40 drops
Pinch of turmeric powder
Gum tragacanth in powder – 1oz
Arrowroot 8oz
Rice in powder – 8oz

Mix thoroughly and pass through a sieve.

medicines to soothe teething babies contained morphine; and tonics often had a high alcohol content. People often had no idea what they were consuming. Nevertheless, the makers of many proprietary medicines achieved huge financial success in the eighteenth and nineteenth centuries. Clarke's Blood Mixture, for example, survived in its original formula from 1861 to 1909 and asserted that it was a *guaranteed* cure for 'all blood diseases', including 'Scrofula, Scurvy, Glandular Swellings and Sores, Cancerous Ulcers, Bad Legs, Syphilis, Piles, Rheumatism, Gout, Dropsy, Blackheads or Pimples of the Face and Sore Eyes.' (After 1909, the formula was improved, and it was finally withdrawn only in the 1960s.)

The notion that one medicine would treat everything was very seductive and cure-alls made the most outlandish claims; Dr Martins Miraclettes promised that 'Whatever you may be suffering from do not worry or fear, as Dr Martins Miraclettes will be a certain cure for you! Dr Martins Miraclettes make the weak and sickly become strong and healthy, and the aged become youthful and full of energy.' All manner of products were sold, from perfumes and laxatives to fly papers - even Japanese Cheroots, which, according to the manufacturers, could prevent cholera, and were 'so mild that they could be used by the fair sex without causing nausea'.

One of the most successful was Dr Collis Browne's Chlorodyne, which he is thought to have compounded in the late 1840s while serving in the British Army in India. The medicine was phenomenally popular; its reputation spread by word of mouth rather than advertising and it was used to treat everything from coughs and colds to hysteria, cholera and dysentery. Many proprietary medicines were next to useless, but Chlorodyne brought considerable relief. This is perhaps not surprising when you consider that a one ounce bottle (30 ml) contained 12 doses of morphia and 36 of chloroform. The product is still produced today – though it is now only available on prescription.

But the notion that a medicine was compounded by a physician was not a guarantee of an effective remedy. Dr James' Fever powders, developed in the mid-eighteenth century, were designed to treat fevers by inducing sweating and vomiting and were used until the early twentieth century. The product contained antimony which is poisonous and can be fatal when consumed in excess. Still worse was Fowler's Solution which contained arsenic, but which was used to treat everything from worms to asthma and typhus to syphilis.

☠ *Opium soothing drink* ☠

Sydenham's laudanum 30 grammes
Ether (0.735) 15 grammes
Water 1000 grammes

☠ *Children's Cough Syrup* ☠

Ipecacuanha Wine 3 fl. drs
Spirit of Chloroform 1½ fl. drs
Spirit of Nitrous Ether 1½ fl. drs
Solution of ammonium Acetate 4 fl. drs
Syrup of Tolu 6 fl. drs
Solution of cochineal 1 fl. dr.
Syrup to 6 fl. oz.

Jesse Boot was phenomenally successful and within a few years he opened a warehouse and factory. A girl who worked in the packing room in 1890 recalled that she worked from 8 a.m. to 7 p.m. with a break of one hour for lunch. The day was spent packing the aforementioned lobelia pills, bronchial lozenges, flower of sulphur and one ounce boxes of herbs by hand.

Errand boy Bob Elliott was employed by Boot on 16 March 1881, aged not quite 11. He recalled that the shops were terribly busy:

From 10.30 to 12 most of the village carriers would come with their general orders to be assembled ready for the carriers calling later, or to be sent to their carts. Between 10.30 and 12.30 the 'swell' shoppers arrived in large numbers, using horse drawn carriages. … There would be a good sprinkling of farmers and that type of customer, also town people, making a crowd which filled the shop until about 12.30. From 12.30 to about two o'clock business was a bit quieter, not enough to allow the staff to leave the shop for a mid-day meal, but enough to allow them to get something to eat on the premises in relays. Then, on again, busier than ever … up to about four o'clock or a little later.

Elliott observed that this was the quietest part of the day:

the staff could leave the shop in batches for three quarters of an hour, which meant the chance for a substantial meal and so ready for the evening's rush, which was as fierce as anything during the day and comprised mostly town people. By nine o'clock things were quieter, but certainly enough for the tired assistants. When closing time came at 10 or 10.30 the most pleasing thought was that the next day was Sunday!

Jesse Boot was keen to point out that he greatly valued his pharmacists and treated then better than most. In 1893, he said:

We have several qualified men with us, who have come to us from the service of firms where they worked 14 hours daily … and had to be on call on Sundays. With us the daily hours are much shorter; there is a complete half-holiday weekly; there is no Sunday duty; and we make arrangements to send qualified relief every year to enable assistants to have a holiday.

Boot did not open a dispensary until 1884. The Pharmacy Act of 1868 allowed only registered persons to sell or keep a shop for retailing, dispensing or compounding poisons and to use the title of chemist, druggist or pharmacist. Boot was not qualified and prohibited from employing a chemist, but he observed that department stores – limited liability companies – were able to do so, much to the fury of the Pharmaceutical Society which unsuccessfully tried to stop the practice. Boot converted his business into a limited liability company in 1883 and employed a chemist, George Waring, who adopted the company hard-sell tactics; the usual charge for a prescription was 2s. 6d, but Waring charged half that sum. He was rapidly put in charge of recruiting more chemists to work in other branches – it was clear that being able to professionally dispense medicines gave an air of solid respectability to the rest of the profitable over-the-counter products.

Boot's approach to marketing was to sell large quantities of goods at lower prices than his rivals; success was dependent on achieving a high turnover. He took out an advertisement in the *Nottingham Daily Express*, offering 'Patent Medicines Retail At Wholesale Prices' and listing the prices of 128 items – and he doubled his trade. He advertised for a number of months until he had established himself as the largest seller of off-the-shelf medicines in the district and bargain-hunters formed long queues outside his branches.

☠ *Diarrhœa Mixture* ☠

Aromatic Sulphuric Acid 15 fl. drs
Tincture of Chloroform and Morphine
(B.P. 1885) 10 fl. drs

Lovage Infusion

Instant relief for an upset stomach.

———◦•◦———

Dried lovage (Levisticum officinale) seeds 1 teaspoon
Brandy 3 tablespoons
Golden granulated sugar to taste

Put the lovage seeds into the brandy and leave to infuse for 10-20 minutes. Strain the infusion and discard the seeds, sweeten with sugar before drinking.

Peppermint Tisane

Take as a digestive and to ease headaches.

———◦•◦———

Fresh mint leaves 2-3 teaspoons (or half measures if using dried

Bring one pint of water to the boil, pour over the leaves and leave to stand for three to eight minutes. Strain and discard the leaves before drinking.

Compound Tincture of Cardamoms 20 fl. drs
Decoction of Logwood to 60 fl. oz.

THE INSIDE OF A SHOP

The key to the success of any pharmacist, chemist or druggist was in ensuring the public knew what they were selling. This is not as straightforward as it might seem: in 1830, only 50 per cent of the population had basic literacy skills, so it was vital for chemists to supply an immediate visual aid that identified their trade.

An apothecary's premises bore more of a resemblance to a doctor's surgery, with a dispensing area fitted out with drug jars, unlike the chemist with its artful displays. Before the introduction of plate glass in the 1830s, the chemist's shop windows were made of small squares of glass. Behind these were shelves packed with a variety of bottles and jars, which left the interior as dark and as full of promise as Aladdin's cave. Tall storage bottles, known as carboys and filled with richly coloured liquid, always formed a central part of the window display. These had been used by apothecaries and physicians since the 1600s for identification purposes and were adopted by chemists and druggists. Any old colour would not do: producing a successful mix, which would not fade in the sun, was probably one of the first preparations a new chemist undertook.

3oz Nickel sulphate
6oz sulphuric acid
2 gallons water

Dissolve the nickel sulphate in the water and add the acid, stirring constantly. Allow to deposit and decant.

Red

3dr. Iodine
3 dr. Potassium iodide
10oz Hydrochloric acid
2 gallons water

Dissolve the iodide and potassium iodide in 8oz of water and dilute with the rest to which the acid has been added.

Blue

4 oz or more copper sulphate
A sufficiency of solution of ammonia
2 gallons of water

Dissolve the copper sulphate in 2 gallons of water and add the solution of ammonia with constant stirring until the precipitate is redissolved, then add the rest of the water.

Amethyst

10 gr Sodium salicylate
½ dr. Tincture of ferric chloride
2 gallons water

Dissolve the sodium salicylate in the water and add the tincture.

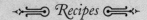

Recipes

Liquid Rouge

Provides a subtle glow for the cheeks.

———

Rectified spirit (such as vodka) 2 oz
Distilled water 6 oz
Cochineal powder 1 oz

Mix the spirit and water, then infuse the cochineal in 3 oz of the mixture and steep for 15 minutes at 100 degrees Fahrenheit. Set aside until cold. Pour off the coloured liquor and repeat the process with another 3 oz of the mixture and then again with the last 2 oz. Finally mix all together, filter and make the filtrate up to 8 oz by pouring distilled water over the contents of the filter.

The focal point of the shop was the counter, which might also serve as a dispensing bench in smaller shops, where the pharmacist would work in full view. In larger shops, a special room was dedicated to dispensing. In this stood a brass beam scale, which was used to weigh large quantities of powder. For small accurate measurements, equal arm scales were used. These had small weights, shaped like coins, which were stored in a front drawer and measured weight in drachms, the standard measurement for powders. Precise measurements were a matter of life and death, and chemists could not afford to make mistakes. The trade magazine of the day, *The Chemist & Druggist*, alerted readers to mishaps, enabling readers to avoid making the same mistake.

The interior of the shop was dominated by the counter, the drawers underneath and the drug run – a set of drawers, each with its own label, containing powdered chemicals, herbs and roots, all made from polished mahogany. A mortar and pestle had pride of place on top of the counter and was in constant use, crushing, grinding and mixing the herbs and drugs. Mortar and pestles were made from a variety of materials, but all had to be hard enough to crush a substance while at the same time being impervious to it.

The raw ingredients, herbs and minerals, were decanted for use from huge sacks kept in a storeroom at the rear. There was a vast array of elaborate containers, known as shop rounds, to display the stock in store. Powders were popped into wide necked bottles, to make it easy to extract the contents, but liquid medicines were put into narrow necked bottles, to make pouring precise doses manageable. Oils were stored in bottles with a tiny spout in the neck and all designs were topped with glass stoppers. Syrups were the exception: the contents were so sticky that glass stoppers would glue tight with use; tin caps were used instead, though these could stick too.

☠ *Soothing Syrup or Mother's Friend* ☠

Bicarbonate of potass 3 teaspoons
Turkey rhubarb root 1 ounce
Cinnamon bark 1 ounce
Loaf sugar 1 pound

Boil in one pint of water twenty minutes, cool, strain, and add two pints of peppermint water and ten drops of oil of cassia or cinnamon. The necessity has long been seen of possessing a simple vegetable remedy without having to resort to infants' preservative, anodyne cordials, royal mixture, &c., &c., the principle ingredients of which are powerful poisons acting on the nervous system. This soothing syrup is purely vegetable, containing no narcotic or poisonous drugs, removing acidity of the stomach, griping pains of the bowels, expelling wind, changing the colour of the motions from a green and slimy appearance to their natural colour. Give from half a teaspoonful to a teaspoon four times a day.

BOTTLES AND CONTAINERS

Volatile substances, such as ether, vaporise at low temperatures and cause stoppers to blow. To overcome this problem, ether bottles were designed with a close-fitting dome on top of the stopper. If the stopper blew, the pressure would be released, but the dome would force the stopper to drop back into position.

Bottles containing poison were coloured to help the illiterate recognise the danger, although the system was not infallible. Blue was the original colour for poison bottles, but this changed to green in the middle of the nineteenth century. Some chemists popped sandpaper collars over poison bottles, or tied

Glass bottles with stoppers, known as shop rounds, were used to store liquids. The design of bottle necks and stoppers was altered for materials such as syrups, oils and volatile liquids.

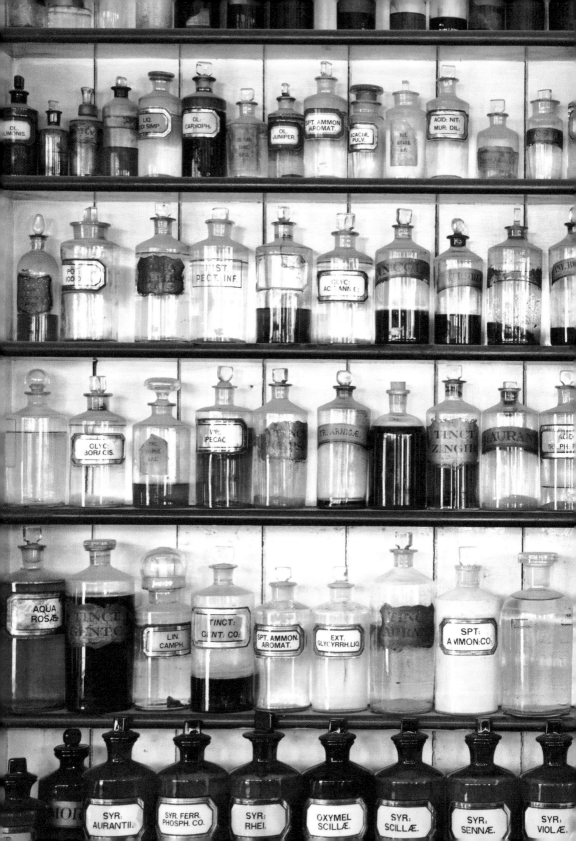

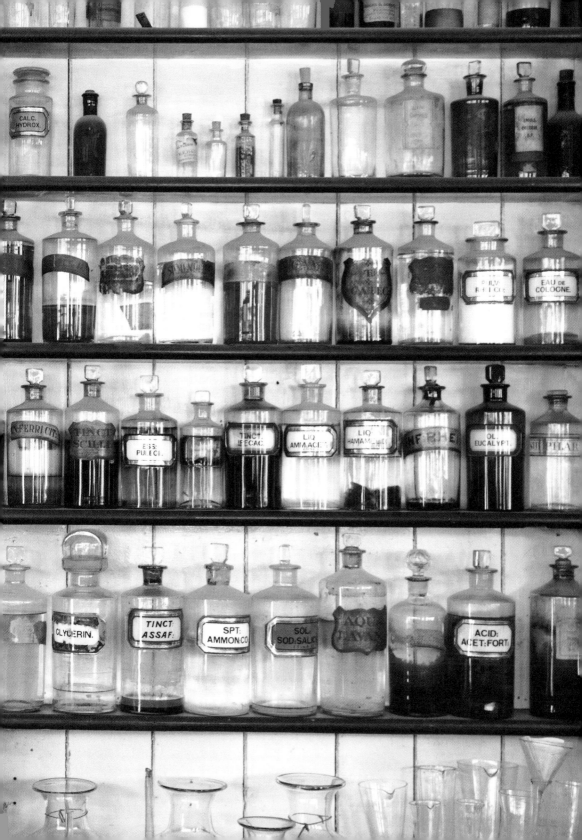

bells around the neck to act as alerts. Later in the century, ridged bottles were used for poisons to provide immediate tough warning of the toxic contents.

As the century wore on, medicine was sold in larger quantities, so bottles were introduced with grooved markers to indicate the number of individual doses it contained. Even so, there were many reported cases of accidental poisonings due to bad packaging, poor labelling and illiteracy. All the labels of dispensed medicines were handwritten in black ink. The labels of poison bottles were in red. Everything else had gold labels with red borders. Labels were often varnished once they had been stuck in place, to help preserve them from wear and tear. Listing the ingredients contained within a medicine was not compulsory. Indeed many formulations were secret, to secure business. Even when a contents list was supplied, it was in Latin. But what went into a medicine was of little interest to the public: anything that had spectacular effect, notably anything that caused vomiting or diarrhoea, was deemed to be worth the money. If the patient got better, the medicine was credited with the cure. A label from the Boots archive reveals the thinking behind another popular blend:

Herbal Smoking Mixtures to strengthen the lungs. Smokers who have tried the compound declare it to be deliciously fragrant, slightly exhilarating and withal, soothing to the nerves. Doctors recommend it.

Ointments and creams were made in bulk and stored in large, decorative earthenware or stoneware jars.

LEECHES AND BLOOD-LETTING

Live medicinal leeches were a standard item of stock; these were kept in special, highly decorative, leech jars made of creamware or earthenware. The jar had a perforated lid to prevent the leeches escaping and to allow air to circulate. Leeches can survive in a dilute saline solution for up to a year without feeding. When looking for the best leeches to sell, the chemist looked for those swimming fastest because these were the hungriest. Smaller jars were sold for transporting leeches; these had a metal clip to help keep the lid in place and prevent accidental spillage.

Leeches were procured via salesmen who specialised in their trade. Until the middle of the nineteenth century, the leech was used enthusiastically to treat almost any illness from dysentery to nymphomania. Some people liked to be bled every year in the spring as a matter of course. Much of the bleeding was a pointless exercise at best, and at worst hazardous to the already weakened sick. Nevertheless, in cases of inflammation and localised swelling, it would have been an effective treatment. Philippe-Frédéric Blandin used leeches in 1836 to restore circulation after reconstructing a patient's nose.

Leeches are 5–10 cm (2–4 in) long and have three jaws specifically designed to draw blood. Each jaw is a muscular organ with about 100 teeth. The arrangement of jaws produces a neat y-shaped cut that leaves little tissue damage but gives the leech access to the underlying blood vessels. It feeds by attaching its head sucker onto the skin. Salivary ducts between the teeth release a strong local anaesthetic that makes the bite painless. As it sucks, it releases a powerful anti-coagulant that prevents the blood from clotting; a vasodilator, which opens up the blood vessels; and a spreading agent that moves the chemicals right across the bite. The proteins and enzymes that have this effect have been isolated and are currently being utilised in the development of drugs to treat cardiovascular disease and

Recipes

Elderflower Ointment

A cooling ointment for any inflammation.

Prepared lard 6 lb

Suet ½ lb

Freshly gathered flowers free from stalks 1 lb

Melt the lard with the suet, add the flowers and heat to a temperature of about 140 degrees Fahrenheit for three hours. Strain, press and filter through a hot funnel.

osteoarthritis. But there is still no drug that can duplicate the effect of a leech bite and, therefore, leeches are utilised today in microsurgery where the intent is to encourage bleeding to benefit circulation, rather than stopping it.

Leeching was generally regarded as one of the least painful methods of bleeding; the leech feeds for about 20 minutes, swells as it feeds, then drops off when bloated. It removes only about two teaspoons of blood (5 ml) at a time while feeding. Because of the anti-coagulants, though, the wound continues to bleed for up to 10 hours, during which time around 150ml (5 fl oz) of blood will be lost. Blood-letting, which was often done by a barber, involved opening the vein to remove a large quantity of blood. For this, chemists sold sets of specially designed knives.

Blood-letting was to finally lose its place as a cure from the 1850s onwards. In America, doctors concluded that blood-letting, and the use of mercury in preparations such as calomel, had debilitated the population, particularly the female population. The American author Thomas Wentworth Higginson (1823–1911) wrote in 1861:

> *In this country it is scarcely an exaggeration to say that every man grows to manhood surrounded by a circle of invalid relatives, that he later finds himself the husband of an invalid wife and the parent of invalid daughters, and that he comes at last to regard invalidism as the normal creation of that sex – as if Almighty God did not know how to create a woman.*

PHYSIC GARDEN

In addition to collecting wild plants for use in herbal remedies, the enterprising chemist planted his own physic garden. It was common practice to separate the plants with wood or brick dividers, and everything was carefully marked with labels. A standard selection included the fragrant angelica, which

A wood engraving from 1877 shows a misunderstanding between a doctor and his confused patient who has swallowed the leeches prescribed for bleeding. ☞

OH, HORROR!

Surgeon. "YOUR PULSE IS STILL VERY HIGH, MY FRIEND! DID YOU GET THOSE LEECHES ALL RIGHT I SENT THE DAY BEFORE YESTERDAY?"

Patient. "YES, SIR, I GOT 'EM RIGHT ENOUGH. BUT MIGHTN'T I HAVE 'EM BILED NEXT TIME, SIR?"

was used to sooth flatulence and indigestion. The herb was also prescribed as a tonic to treat colds, and as a natural sweetener. Herbal infusions of chamomile flowers were taken to soothe stomach ulcers, used as gargles for mouth ulcers and as fragrant hair rinses to lighten and brighten blonde hair. Comfrey was one of the foremost medical herbs; the powdered root was used in compresses to treat, cuts, ulcers, bruises and sprains.

Fennel relieved the symptoms of heartburn and constipation as well as easing the symptoms of cystitis. Feverfew was a common treatment for nervous disorders and was popped into a poultice to soothe insect bites and stings. Garlic was the main ingredient of Four Thieves Vinegar, drunk by robbers of dead plague victims as protection against the disease. Juniper featured in steam inhalations designed to treat coughs, colds and catarrh and juniper foot baths were believed to relieve the pain of arthritis and rheumatism.

Putting aside its obvious use as a perfume, lavender was said to ease digestive complaints, and was popped in herb pillows to aid sleep. Lemon balm was treated as a sedative and also used to relieve flatulence. The soothing and healing herb marigold was a standard feature in ointment and cream mixtures designed to soothe wounds and sore spots. Marshmallow was also soothing and healing, though with different functions; infusions of the roots were used to quieten coughs and to overcome insomnia.

Parsley was used in a mass of concoctions, to treat everything from bad breath to head lice. Mustard was commonly used in poultices to relieve the pain and inflammation of rheumatism and also as an emetic. Like so many other herbs, rosemary was regarded as a digestive aid and was thought to ease flatulence. It was also used as a mouthwash and a hair rinse for those with red or dark hair. Sage tea was a treatment for convalescents, to aid digestion and for sore throats, sore gums and mouth ulcers. Sage and vinegar poultices were common treatments for sprains and bruising; the vinegar brings the bruise to the surface and reducing swelling while the sage soothes and heals. Thyme, a tonic and stimulant, was commonly used in toothpastes and mouthwashes and was thought to be helpful in relieving respiratory infections.

WEIGHTS AND MEASURES

Pharmacist recipes were cloaked in secrecy. Anyone without training finds them impossible to decipher. Apothecary symbols were used to represent various units of weights, and roman numerals to detail the amounts required. This in itself would not have been a problem, but there was no consistency. As the recipes scattered throughout this book reveal, some are written with apothecary weights, some use imperial measures, apothecary symbols feature or the weight written in longhand. They might write with the Arab numeral system we use today (1, 2, 3, etc.), they might use Roman numerals (i, ii, iii, etc.). They might write the common name for a compound (horseradish) or the Latin name *(Armoracia rusticana)*.

Pharmacists traditionally worked from two sets of balances. One dealt with smaller weights up to 2 ounces, the other was used for larger quantities up to 2 pounds in weight. Apothecaries had used the Troy weight system for medicinal products from as early as 1270. The Weights and Measures Act of 1858 formally adopted the Avoirdupois (Imperial measure) system, but even then there was not consistency. Metric weight and measures were legalised for use in Britain in 1897, but their use was not widespread.

THE FEMALE PHARMACIST

Pharmacists were usually men, women were not allowed to train until 1879, and even then were expected to give up work on marrying. Before then, there were some registered women pharmacists, but usually only because they had taken over businesses

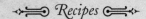

Recipes

Sage and Vinegar Poultice

Used to bring bruises to the surface; the sage soothes and heals.

———◆———

Handful of fresh sage leaves
Cider or wine vinegar

Run a rolling pin over the leaves to bruise them, put the leaves into a pan and cover with vinegar and heat for five minutes without boiling. Remove the leaves and out them on to a a muslin cloth, apply to the affected area as hot as the patient can stand. Cover with towels to retain heat and leave in place for half an hour.

Apothecary Weights

The basic measure of this system was the grain:

gr. *One grain*
 Э *One scruple - 20 grains*
З *One drachm - 60 grains*
Ʒ *One ounce - 480 grains*
℔ *One pound (12 ounces) – 5760 grains*

The liquid grain was introduced in 1885, indicating the volume equivalent of one grain, but it was not widely used. The liquid measures detailed below were favoured and the chemist had an array of large and small glass and ceramic measures.

1 fluid drachm – 1 teaspoon
2 fluid drachms – 1 dessertspoonful
½ fluid ounce – 1 tablespoonful

Imperial Weights (Avoirdupois)

lb *One Pound – 16 oz*
oz *One ounce – 437.5 grains*
one sixteenth of an ounce – 27.3 grains

Imperial Measures

C *One gallon – 8 pints*
O *One pint – 20 fluid ounces*
Ʒ *One fluid ounce – 8 fluid drachms*
З *One fl. Drachm – 60 minims*
♏ *One minim*

established by their husbands or fathers. The Pharmacy Act of 1868 stipulated that all practising pharmacists must be registered with the Pharmaceutical Society. The total number of registered pharmacists in 1869 was 11,638, and of these just 223 were women, just 1.9 per cent of the total. Curiously, this figure fell after 1879: in 1905, there were only 195 female pharmacists on the register, just 1.2 per cent of the 15,948 listed.

Alice Vickery (1844–1929) was the first woman to qualify as a chemist and druggist in 1873, and she had to study in France since British medical schools would not admit women. Even after she qualified, she was not allowed to become a member of the Pharmaceutical Society and therefore had no say in the regulation of the profession until 1879.

☠ *Frost Bite Pencil* ☠

Paraffin ℨix.
Olive oil ℨiiss
Camphor Ʒj.
Iodine Ʒj.
Spirit ℨij

Rub the camphor and iodine up to a fine powder with sufficient spirit and add the olive oil mix and put over gentle heat to melt. When melted add the paraffin, pour into moulds to set. The pencil is to be used night and morning.

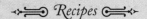

Recipes

Dandruff Lotion

For the relief of a flaky scalp prone to dandruff.

———•·•———

Glycerine, pure 8 oz
Tincture of capsicum 2 oz
Distilled water 25 oz
Eau de Cologne 25 oz

Mix the ingredients together and apply daily with a sponge.

Nettle Hair Rinse

To help eradicate dandruff and leave hair shiny and soft.

———•·•———

Large handful of fresh nettle leaves – wear gloves to protect your skin

Put the leaves into a pan, add 1 pint of water and simmer gently for 15 minutes. Strain and use as a final hair rinse.

VIRTUE'S
HOUSEHOLD
PHYSICIAN

VIRTUE'S
HOUSEHOLD
PHYSICIAN

THE
MODERN
HOME
PHYSICIAN

A TWENTIETH
CENTURY
MEDICA

A TWENTIETH
CENTURY
MEDICA

PRACTICAL
PHARMACY

LUCAS

VOL. II.

VOLUME
TWO

VOLUME
ONE

VIRTUE & CO.

VIRTUE & CO.

CHAPTER 4

———◆———

POISON

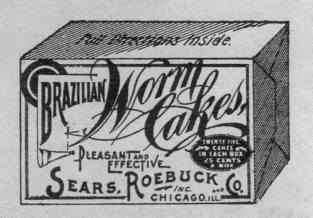

'Poisons and medicine are oftentimes the same substance given with different intents.'

PETER MERE LATHAM (ENGLISH PHYSICIAN AND EDUCATOR)

Toxic ingredients made up a large part of the chemist's stock-in-trade. Many medicines are poisonous in excessive quantities, but are therapeutic taken in small doses – aspirin and paracetamol are two classic examples. Today, poisonous substances are tightly controlled, but there was a much more *laissez-faire* attitude during the reign of Victoria. A number of toxic substances were available, including arsenic, belladonna, opium, laudanum, oxalic acid, nux vomica, antimony and ergot. Controls on the sale and use of poisons were eventually brought in, a direct response not only to murders committed by poisoning but also to the number of accidental deaths.

It should be emphasised that in the first half of the nineteenth century physicians and apothecaries had very little idea of the causes of the illnesses they were trying to treat. Their treatments therefore were generally little more than useless, perhaps with the notable exception of South African tree bark cinchona, of which quinine is a component, and opium. Laudanum (the tincture of opium) and calomel (mercurous chloride) were the two most commonly prescribed drugs at the beginning of the nineteenth century.

Patients who were sick needed strong constitutions, for many of the medicinal remedies would have left them feeling considerably worse. Fowler's solution, which contained arsenic, was used to treat asthma. Tartar emetic, which contains antimony, was used as an emetic with horribly spectacular results. In minute amounts, it acted as a sedative or expectorant, and was found in a once popular remedy for croup – Cox's Hive Syrup. Calomel was commonly given as a purgative and was used long term in the treatment of syphilis. It is a mercury compound that causes salivation, ulceration of the mouth and loss of teeth, and yet it was also used in teething powders, soap and skin-lightening products. Louisa May Alcott (1832–1888), the author

This is my appearance after a good dose of ARSENIC *taken* medicinally.

An illustration from the 1850s shows that there was some understanding that the medicinal use of arsenic was not to be recommended.

of *Little Women*, was treated with calomel after contracting typhoid in 1863 and is said never to have recovered from the effects of her 'cure'.

The most common cause of trouble, though, was arsenic. Its presence in human tissue can be determined, thanks to the Marsh Test, first published in 1836. But it can easily be slipped into food deliberately without attracting attention because it has no taste or smell. This made it the murderer's weapon of choice: the symptoms of arsenic poisoning resemble those of a stomach upset. Newspapers were full of lurid tales of poisoning, often involving women who killed their husbands or lovers. Children were also victims, sometimes because the parents simply could not afford another mouth to feed. In addition, the Friendly Societies paid out for the costs of a funeral, and it was not unknown for children, or partners, to be killed for financial gain. Mary Ann Cotton is the most notorious example: she used arsenic to murder many of her 15 children and stepchildren, as well as three husbands and a fiancé. It is believed that her final tally was 21 deaths. In each case, the arsenic was probably a straightforward over-the-counter purchase. Cotton was sentenced to death and hung on 24 March 1873.

HUMBUG BILLY

The lack of taste and smell, which made arsenic so alluring to the murderer, meant that it could also be taken by accident, especially because it resembles both sugar and flour, although it is also gritty. Arsenic was cheap, at two pence (2d) per ounce – enough to kill huge numbers of vermin or, indeed, people.

Throughout the Victorian era, there were cases of druggists and grocers mistaking arsenic for arrowroot, magnesia, chalk powder or even talcum powder – all with fatal results for their customers.

The worst case of accidental poisoning was the case of the Bradford poisonings in 1858. Joseph Neal was a wholesale confectioner who wanted to make a batch of peppermint creams. It was common practice at the time to adulterate foodstuffs with daft, an inert substance that was low in cost and used in place of a more expensive ingredient. The content of daft was variable: it might be plaster of Paris, sulphate of lime or powdered limestone. Joseph

Neal sent his lodger, James Archer, to the chemist and druggist Charles Hodgson five miles away in Baildon Bridge to acquire the required daft.

Hodgson the chemist was unwell, but was available. His assistant William Goddard attended to the request and asked his master where the daft was to be found. He was told that it was in a cask in the corner of the stock room, where various items were stored. The assistant found it, weighed out 12lb (5.45 kg) as requested. Unfortunately, what he weighed was not daft at all, but arsenic trioxide.

The peppermint lozenges were prepared by James Appleton, an assistant, using 40 lb (18.2 kg) sugar, 4 lb (1.8 kg) gum and the daft – in this case, arsenic. James felt unwell and sneezed throughout the process. The sweets did not look the same as usual, and took longer to dry. The next day, though, a large batch of the peppermint lozenges (40 lb/18.2 kg) were sold to a market stall trader, William Hardaker, known locally as Humbug Billy. The price was marked down by half a penny per pound from 8d to 7½d because of the unusual colour of the sweets.

On 30 October, market day, Humbug Billy set up stall in the Saturday market. He ate one of the peppermint lozenges and felt unwell, so much so that he had to ask someone to take over his stall. It was later estimated that around 1000 peppermints were sold that day, and the inquest revealed that some of the remaining lozenges contained between 11 and 16 grains of arsenic apiece. The peppermint creams were potentially lethal for just four to five grains of arsenic can kill, less in some instances.

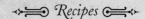

Recipes

Peppermint Lozenges

To freshen the breath.

White sugar 6 oz
Oil of peppermint 36 drops
The whites of 2 eggs

Rub the ingredients together to form a past and make into lozenges.

The sweets did not take long to take effect. Two boys died overnight, and their physician contacted the police, suspecting poisoning. Several more people died the following day, and there were numerous cases of severe gastrointestinal illness. At first an outbreak of cholera was suspected, but it quickly became clear from the number of reports of poisoning coming back from physicians that the sick and dying had all eaten a peppermint from Humbug Billy. The police traced the source of the problem back from Billy, who was ill in bed, to James Neal, and then back to Hodgson the chemist and his assistant Goddard. Goddard showed police the cask he had taken the daft from, and Hodgson realised the mistake.

The police acted quickly, touring public houses and churches to alert the people of the danger, and bell-ringers toured the town. By the Monday morning, notices had been put up throughout the town, warning people of the danger. Nevertheless 12 people had died by midday, and 100 were gravely ill. Furthermore, the neighbouring towns and villages were blissfully unaware of this lethal confectionery, and more people died. In total, 20 people died, mostly children since their lower body mass made them more susceptible to the poison, and 200 people were taken ill.

Neal's lozenges were confiscated. This was no easy task, as the peppermints had been added to mixed selection bags, and a policeman had to sort through them to find the offending articles. He suffered itching of the hands and stinging eyes as a result. Goddard, the chemist's assistant who had accidentally sold the arsenic, was charged with manslaughter on 1 November, shortly after Hodgson the chemist and James Neal, the confectioner, were also committed to trial for the same offence.

The trio were sent to court in York in December 1858. The jury decided that it could not bring about a conviction for manslaughter because there had been no intent to poison; what had happened was a tragic accident. Interestingly, the public seemed to be more infuriated by the realisation that

Pharmacists and their assistants worked long hours, commonly a 12 hour day from Monday to Friday and a 15 hour day on a Saturday. ☞ Following page: Ruth and Nick experiment with the popular Victorian procedure, dry cupping.

VICTORIAN PHARMACY

their food was being adulterated without their knowledge than by the lack of care and attention given to the storage and retail of poison. The Adulteration of Food and Drink Bill was passed in 1860, but The Pharmacy Act, which restricted the sale of drugs to chemists and druggists, was not put onto the statute book until 1868. Even then, there were still cases of accidental poisoning by careless chemists and other unlicensed retailers, who did not want to give up the profitable sale of poisons. The law was not rigidly enforced for many years.

THE CHEMIST'S RESPONSIBILITY

Cases of accidental poisoning were by no means unusual. *The Chemist & Druggist* contained many tragic reports, which served to alert other chemists to the risk. A typical case was covered in the issue of 14 May 1864:

> *On Saturday April 16th, an adjourned inquest was held At Liverpool, relative to the death of Mr John Lingard, a Liverpool tradesman. On the 11th April Mr Lingard, having an cold, received a prescription from Dr Nottingham; the prescription was for a powder consisting of James's powder and Dover's powder and was made up at the shop of Messrs. Clay and Abraham, Bold Street. About half an hour after taking the powder Mr Lingard expired in great agony, the symptoms being those of poisoning by strychnia.*

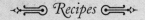

Recipes

Love Hearts

These delicious sweets still remain popular today.

Powdered gum tragacanth
1 teaspoon

Juice of one lemon, or 1 tablespoon rosewater

Icing sugar 2 lb

A few drops of food colouring

Mix the gum tragacanth with the lemon juice or rosewater and leave it to stand for 20 minutes for the gum to swell. It may be a good idea to divide your gloopy mix into several small batches so that you can have each one a different colour. Be sparing with the food colouring – one or two drops will be enough for each batch. Add in the icing sugar until you achieve a semi-firm ball. Next, roll out the mixture very thinly, cut it into rounds and press into a pattern.

After careful analysis by an analytical chemist, the remains of Dover's powders was found, and also strychnine. However, there was no trace of any antimony, which would be expected if James's powders had been consumed. It was established that the prescription had been made up by an assistant of two year's standing, who had made up '50,000 to 60,000' prescriptions. However, it was also noticed that a bottle of strychnine was kept on the same shelf as the James's powders, separated from it by only one other bottle. The jury came to the conclusion that Mr Lingard had come to his death as a result of culpable neglect on the part of the assistant, Richard Poole, who insisted he had made no such error. The verdict was manslaughter, but Mr Poole was released on bail, and Messrs. Clay and Abrahams advised to adopt a better arrangement of their bottles.

The case generated much correspondence in the pages of *The Chemist & Druggist* in defence of the unfortunate chemist. The general view was that the chemist was guilty of 'thoughtlessness', not 'ignorance' and that the case highlighted 'the necessity for all of us to be lenient with our brethren.' Another writer argued that it was the height of criminal injustice to bring a criminal verdict against a man who may be so harassed that he becomes unconscious of what he does and who therefore cannot be held liable for his actions.

Chemists must have found the work mentally and physically demanding. William Gelder, who had undertaken an apprenticeship with a chemist in Edinburgh, wrote to his father in West Yorkshire in March 1834, expressing the difficulties: 'I believe that 6 out of 10 who have served an apprenticeship to a Chemist & Druggist do not like it on account of the tedious hours … requiring very great mental and bodily attention'. Jesse Boot was also aware of the problem. A notice was hung in every dispensing department, warning, 'Accuracy in dispensing depends on the undivided attention of the dispenser.'

The Chemist & Druggist of 15th June 1858 contained a report of an inquest into a child's death. A servant accompanied her mistress's child to the chemist to seek a solution to the child's itch. The chemist supplied a lotion that was to be sponged onto the child's body. The bottle was marked poison. The lotion was applied, the child fell ill and despite his doctor's best efforts, died several days later. The doctor noted excessive salivation, a sign of mercury poisoning; and while mercury was not an unusual remedy for itching, death from mercury poisoning was. At the inquest, after 30 minutes of deliberation, the jury returned the verdict that the cause of death was due to exhaustion from excessive salivation, which in turn was caused by the absorption of mercury into the child's system. The jurors added that they regarded this as an exceptional case, and thought that *some* blame should be attached to the chemist for not supplying more definite written instructions. Indeed the poor chemist was not entirely to blame for the industry was largely unregulated and unpoliced, such *laissez-faire* attitudes were addressed in part, because of the consequences of such tragic accidents.

ARSENIC AS MEDICINE

The Victorians made full use of arsenic's toxic qualities in rat poisons, sheep dip and fly papers. More interestingly, they were also partial to using it as a medicine. In 1783, Thomas Fowler, a Staffordshire physician, had begun treating patients suffering from ague (fever, chills and sweating) with an arsenic-based cure, Fowler's Solution. The results were, apparently, impressive – though this was possibly due to unscientific trials. By 1809, it was commonly prescribed by physicians for all manner of ills, despite its side effects of extreme vomiting and purging, and even though nobody knew what the principal ingredient was. Fowler's Solution was prescribed for all manner of ailments: malaria, asthma, skin problems, rheumatism and even morning sickness!

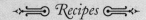

Recipes

Witch Hazel Cream

A soothing emollient cream for sore skin, bruises, stings and swellings.

Anhydrous wool fat 2½ lb

Almond oil 1 pint

Distilled solution of witch hazel 1 pint

Rose otto oil 10 drops

Mix the wool fat and almond oil over a pan of hot water; gradually add the remaining ingredients.

In his book *The Arsenic Century*, James C. Whorton argues that dyspepsia – a term applied to great range of symptoms from indigestion and flatulence to insomnia, anxiety and depression – could have been caused by the overuse of arsenic. Women dipped arsenic fly papers in water and applied the solution to their faces to improve their complexions, and men imbibed it to improve their virility or as a cure for baldness.

A recipe for a skin tonic in *Pharmaceutical Formulas* suggests treating pimples and blackheads internally, and promises to be 'safe and efficacious':

☠ *Liquor Arsenicalis* ☠

Liquor arsenicalis ℥ *xl.*
Potass. Bircarb ʒiss.
Tr. Gent. Co. ℥j.
Tr. Card. Co . ℥ss.
Aq, chloroformii ad ℥viij.

EVERYDAY TOXINS

While the Victorians were shocked by cases of poisoning, whether deliberate or accidental, this did not impair their enthusiasm for toxic substances. They merrily consumed all manner of toxic substances in everyday medicinal and cosmetic preparations. Belladonna was used by women as a beauty aid to dilate the pupils, though prolonged use was said to cause blindness. It was also used for apparently more straightforward reasons: In Louisa M. Alcott's *Little Women*, Beth cares for a sick baby. When it dies of scarlet fevers she is instructed by the doctor to 'go home and take belladonna right away'. Mercury compounds were used in the popular patent medicine Calomel. Antimony, a deadly poison, was used as an emetic as well as in Dr James's Fever Powder. And Dr J. Collis Browne's Chlorodyne contained chloroform (highly addictive), ether and morphia. In fact, some recipes for Chlorodyne included cannabis, making for a potent cocktail of drugs.

Belladonna has a long history of use as a cosmetic, a poison and a medicine.

☠ *Chlorodyne* ☠

*Many recipes have been given for this, Mr Groves gives the following
as an improvement on the recipe of Dr Ogden.*

Take chloroform 4drs.
Ether 1½ drs.
Oil of peppermint 8 drs.
Resin of Indian Hemp 16 grs.
Capsicum 2grs.

Macerate for 2–3 days and filter.
Then dissolve hydrochlorate of morphia 16 grs. in 1 fl oz of syrup
*Add perchloric acid and water, half dr each, assisting the solution
by a water-bath, then, when cold, add hydrocyanic acid (Scheele's)
96 drops. Mix the solution. Should be given with great caution.*

Many of the proprietary medicines sold off the shelf were highly addictive. Laudanum, an opium tincture and potent narcotic, was one of the most commonly abused medicines. Nurses spoon-fed it to their charges; it was taken for colds and as a painkiller. It was abused by the working classes, being cheaper than gin or wine. The list of famous users is legendary, including Elizabeth Barrett Browning (1806–1861); Lizzie Sidall (1829–1862), the pre-Raphaelite model and wife of the painter Rossetti; Branwell Brontë, brother of the three sisters; Florence Nightingale (1820–1910); and Louisa May Alcott. Some people were alert to the danger and purchased medicines such as 'Gare's Universal Cough Cure – Free from Opium'.

During this time, the properties of cannabis were also being explored, as the *Companion to the British Pharmacopeia of 1864* reveals:

☠ *Cannabis Indica* ☠
Indian Hemp

The flowering tops of the female plant of the Cannabis sativa, *from which the resin has not been removed, dried. Cultivated in India.*

We are indebted to Dr. O'Shaugnessy for the first introduction of Indian Hemp in this country. He bought over a quantity with him from India, which the author converted into extract for him, and distributed amongst a large number of the profession under Dr. O'Shaughnessy's directions.

Medicinal Properties.

Dr. Glendenning used It largely, and his opinion is as follows:- 'It acts as a soporific or hypnotic in conciliating sleep, as an anodyne in lulling irritation; as an antispasmodic in checking cough and cramp, as a nervine stimulant in removing languor and anxiety, and raising the pulse and spirits without any drawback or deduction on account of indirect or incidental inconveniences, producing tranquil sleep without causing constipation, nausea or other effect or sign of indigestion, without headache or stupor.'

Preparations.

EXTRACTUM.

Indian Hemp, in coarse powder, 1; Rectified spirit, 5: macerate seven days, press and evaporate.

Dose.- ¼ to 1 gr. In pill.'

Following page: Pharmacists sold many medicines for livestock as well as humans, here Professor Nick Barber makes up his own horse embrocation. ☞

CHAPTER 5

POTIONS, POWDERS, PERFUMES AND PILLS

'The desire to take medicine is perhaps the greatest feature which distinguishes man from animals.'

SIR WILLIAM OSLER (PHYSICIAN 1849 - 1919)

he Victorian pharmacy was nothing if not labour-intensive. Aside from the proprietary medicines and products offered by the chemist, every single item was handmade. Each suppository, pill, tablet, capsule, lozenge and cachet (an individual dose of powdered medicine sandwiched into a rice paper packet) was created by the chemist and his assistants. Chemists would have a go at making anything that was required: nostrums (family herbal remedies passed down through the generations), indigestion powders, elixirs, blister plasters, corpulence cures, sleeping pills, toothpaste, tonics, perfume and soap.

These men were often at the forefront of scientific development, directing their natural interest and curiosity in the subject towards the development of crude drugs. The German chemist Friedrich Gaedcke (1828–1890) isolated cocaine from coca leaves, using a method developed by Friedrich Sertürner (1783–1841), a chemist's assistant. Noticing that different batches of opium varied in their narcotic effect, Sertürner was the first person to isolate the active ingredient associated with a plant or herb. Similar investigations into the active ingredient from willow bark eventually led to the creation of aspirin in 1893, by Felix Hoffman (1868–1946), who worked for Bayer. The drug was launched in 1899, and it is estimated that 100 billion tablets are now swallowed every year.

The production of drugs and medicines was a painstaking business. First the chemist had to ensure that all the required ingredients were available and then that they were properly prepared for use. This was physical, repetitive work: leaves, stems and roots had to be sliced (root-cutting machines could

An illustration from 1820 shows the interior of a chemist shop: the pharmacist serves the customer while his young apprentice works away with the pestle and mortar. ☞

help to take the strain) and many substances had to be reduced to a powder with a mortar and pestle. Powders often required sifting to ensure that the desired particle size was achieved, and the chemist had a selection of sieves with graded mesh sizes to ensure quality control. The pestle and mortar, or a fine grater such as we use for nutmeg, was also used to bruise ingredients.

POWDERS

The simplest dosage for chemists to produce was a powder; ingredients were pounded using a pestle and mortar and thoroughly mixed together. Individual doses were carefully weighed and then wrapped up in paper. Mr Kendrick, a former Boots employee at the turn of the century, remembered the popularity of single doses in Nottingham:

> *During this period, there were many people living in that area, who were very poor indeed, living under slum conditions. If they were 'under the weather', as they often were, especially after the usual night drinking bouts, they would go to 'Jesse's' for a 'haporth or pennorth' of Salts [Epsom Salts]. This was CURE for their stomach upsets.'*

Victorian pharmacist scales were things of beauty, with specially designed wooden boxes containing portable scales and a range of tiny weights. Following page: Most items stocked by the pharmacist were handmade and assistants spent the bulk of their time grinding basic ingredients.

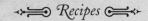

Recipes

Almond Wash Powder

A good cleanser for the skin that is less irritating than pure soap.

———

Almond powder 16 oz

Rice flour 2 oz

Powdered soap 1 oz

Orris root powder 1 oz

Bergamot oil (or perfumed oil of choice) 6 drops or to taste

Combine the dry ingredients and then add a few drops of bergamot oil, or other perfume of your choice. The powder can then be used as a soap substitute.

An advertisement from The Chemist & Druggist *lures pharmacists to purchase ready-made pearl coated pills.*

Epsom Salts, originally obtained from a mineral spring in Epsom, were artificially created from a mix of powdered magnesium, sulphur and oxygen. It was a common remedy for disorders of the stomach and bowls, but was also used in bath salts, to treat boils and soothe tired feet, while a small dose (½ teaspoon) popped into chicken food daily was said to prevent stomach upsets in poultry.

The downside to this most basic form of medication was that many of the powders tasted vile. A way around this was to put the powder into the centre of a small wafer of rice paper, moisten it at the edges, then attach another circle of rice paper on top. The chemist did not have to cut their own rounds from sheets of rice paper – they could purchase the wafers ready cut. Cachets were similar to wafers, the only difference being that a special machine used pressure to seal the edges of the paper. The customer would then dip the cachet into water and swallow it.

Not all powders were for oral consumption: medicated powders for skin problems, fragrant powders for dusting and face powders for cosmetic use were all manufactured by the chemist.

PILLS

The first step in making a pill was to weigh out the active ingredients. A formula gave the weight of each of the active ingredients required to make one pill; the chemist would them multiply this by the number of pills he needed to make.

The active ingredients were ground into a fine powder using a pestle and mortar. The next stage was

Recipes

Perspiration Powder

Helps to relieve excessive perspiration.

Carbolic acid 1 part
Oil of lemon 2 parts
French chalk 4 parts
Burnt alum 4 parts
Powdered starch 200 parts

Mix thoroughly and pass through a sieve. To be sprinkled in the gloves or stockings or applied to the hands or feet.

to add an active substance to bind the ingredients; liquid glucose was commonly used, added just one drop at a time until a stiff, workable mixture was formed. An early device to form the pills was called a 'pill tile'; the mixture was rolled first into a ball and then into a long sausage. This could then be divided and cut into the number of pills, which were then rolled into a spherical shape between the finger and thumb. The final process was to pop the pills into a 'pill rounder', which was moved in a circular motion until the pills achieved a nicely rounded finish. They were then put on one side to dry.

The pills could then be varnished by rolling them in a pot containing resin, or alcohol and ether. For the rich, a gold, silver or pearl coating might be desirable; chemists would put mucilage – a gluey substance – into a Pill Silverer, a specially designed box containing gold leaf, silver leaf or calcium carbonate (for a pearl finish). This box was then rotated until the pills were coated. Later in the nineteenth century, pill machines with brass cutters were invented.

To use these, the mixture was first pounded, ground and rolled in the same way, but then the length of mixture was placed on the lower cutters and the top cutter was moved back and forth, until rough pills rolled into the drawer at the end of the machine. These machines were available in a variety of sizes, from one grain to five grains, to suit the weight of active ingredients required.

It is worth noting that none of these methods were precise, and the active ingredients would not necessarily have been equally distributed throughout the mixture.

TABLETS

Today we interchange the terms pill and tablet, but in fact there is a difference, and not all active ingredients are suitable for production in tablet form. Pills are made by mixing ingredients with liquid adhesive agents (which can render the medicinal compounds ineffective), while tablets are formed by compressing the active ingredients.

Pharmacists required special equipment, here cachet machines designed to envelop nasty tasting powders within edible rice paper wafers. ☞

Making pills was a laborious and painstaking business, the active ingredients had to be carefully weighed and thoroughly mixed to ensure that each pill contained a precise and quantifiable measure.

VICTORIAN PHARMACY

Tablets first made an appearance in the nineteenth century. The first, called a 'compressed pill', was created by William Brockedon (1784–1854) in 1843. He invented a die and punch machine, which is generally thought to have changed the face of medicine. Powder was poured into a tube and then compressed with a mallet until it was solid; the tablet was then punched out.

Tablets did not win immediate approval. In 1895, *The Pharmaceutical Journal* described them as 'one of the evils suffered by legitimate pharmacy', concluding that 'tablets have had their day.' They could not have been more wrong; Brockedon's invention led to the development of more commercial machines that spewed out great quantities of tablets on an industrial scale. In fact, manufacturing chemists took over tablet production in the twentieth century – liberating the dispensing chemist from one of their daily chores.

CAPSULES

Even more complex was the process of making capsules to hold the vilest of liquid medicines. Each capsule had to be individually handmade from olive-shaped moulds, which were dipped into a gelatine solution. The mould was turned until the gelatine dried, then the capsule could be cut from the mould. The process was time-consuming and fiddly. Many chemists preferred to buy ready-made capsules which had a small hole in the top. These convenient devices were filled by injecting the medicine into the capsule with a syringe, then sealing the hole with heat, or by applying more glycerine with a fine brush.

Recipes

Cold Cream

To smooth the skin and for the removal of makeup.

Beeswax 2 oz

Jojoba oil 4 oz

Almond oil 4 oz

Rose water 2 oz

Melt the wax over a pan of boiling water. Remove from the heat and stir in the oils and rosewater. Allow to cool and transfer to a jar.

LOZENGES AND PASTILLES

Lozenges and pastilles (or jujubes) were developed to prolong the delivery of medicine in the mouth and throat regions. They were often used to treat colds, sore throats, catarrh and oral thrush. Traditionally a lozenge is hard and solid right through; it was made by combining the active ingredients in a base of sugar and edible gum, mixed with some distilled water. This mixture was then rolled out, like pastry, to the required thickness; some chemists used lozenge boards to help them achieve a perfect finish. Lozenge cutters were used to cut the shape, which was then popped into an oven for a while to dry out. The finished product could be dusted with sugar to stop it sticking. The following recipe is extracted from Henry Beasley's *The Druggist's General Receipt Book* (1895):

☠ *Ching's Worm Lozenges* ☠

The yellow lozenges contain: 1gr, Calomel in each, with sugar and sufficient mucilage (coloured with saffron) to form a paste. The brown contain half a gr. Of Calomel with 3½ gr of resinous extract of Jalap

Pastilles were jelly-like in consistency: glycerine and gelatine were heated until soft, and then the active ingredients, flavouring and colouring were added. Ready-made shallow, grooved mould trays were available. The warm mixture would be poured in, left to set and then cut, following the groove lines. There were various mould designs, including circular ones. Chemists starting out in business could make temporary moulds by filling a tray with starch, making indents with a round object, and then pouring the pastille mix into these holes. Once the mixture was set, the starch was removed by washing, leaving the pastilles. These would then be coated with sugar and packed in damp-resistant paper.

Cachous were used as breath-freshening sweets. In essence, they were lozenges flavoured with essential oils. Elizabeth Stride, one of the prostitutes murdered by Jack the Ripper, was found clutching a packet in her lifeless hand on 30 September 1888.

Drawn by M.E. Esq.   Pub. Jan.ʸ 8ᵗʰ 1827, by T. Gillard, 46 Strand.

SWALLOWING A PILL.

gup—gup—Gup_!

Medicines were the favoured form of treatment in the nineteenth century. Pills were less popular because they were hard to swallow and tasted vile, although wealthy customers could pay to have them coated to make them less distasteful.

☠ *Cachou Aromatise* ☠

Powdered mace 216 gr.
Powdered cardamoms 154 gr.
Powdered vanilla 283 gr.
Powdered cloves 77 gr.
Powdered orris-root 309 gr.
Oil of neroli 20 drops
Oil of cinnamon 30 drops
Oil of lemon 40 drops
Oil of peppermint 60 drops
Extract of liquorice 2 oz.
Chocolate 3 oz.
Syrup to make a mass.

Divide into small pills and silver.

MEDICINE

Liquid medicines could come in any number of forms and were the most favoured form of medication. Until the mid-nineteenth century, medicine generally consisted of a single draught – just one dose. Either the pharmacist would prepare this, or the medicine might be sold in the form of a dry weight of herbs for the patient to take home and brew up themselves to make a fresh infusion. The method is simple: steep the herb in hot water, strain after around five minutes and drink the strained liquid. Concentrated infusions last longer and were prepared by the chemist. They are made with alcohol, then diluted with water before use.

Medicines could be utilised for all manner of curious ailments. A copy of *The Working Man's Model Botanic Guide to Health*, a book that details the Thomsonian herbal system, was used in Boots in the late nineteenth century. The following entry reveals the medicine and treatment for the *disease* of masturbation.

… We could disclose cases that have come under our notice that would harrow up the feelings of every parent. It produces consumption, and it has been shown by reports of lunatic asylums that it often causes insanity in both sexes. … Let the young take warning, and those that are in danger flee from it. We would advise the young to read Graham's 'Lectures on Chastity' as well as other works. TREATMENT – Abandon the practice immediately, and wash the parts in cold water night and morning …

Bistort root 1 ounce
Priory breava – 1 ounce
Bayberry bark – 1 ounce
White poplar bark – 1 ounce
Gum catechu – 1 ounce

Boil with two quarts of water for half an hour; when cool, clear, and add four ounces of the decoction of sasparilla.
Dose: A wineglassful four times daily

TINCTURES

Tinctures were prepared by removing the active ingredient of a drug by percolation or soaking.

With the right equipment, percolation was a simple operation: the active ingredient was softened

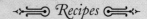

Recipes

Marshmallow Milk

Take one teaspoon three times a day to relieve hoarse coughs.

Freshly grated marshmallow root 1 oz
Milk 1 pint
Honey 1–2 tablespoons, or to taste

Put the marshmallow root and milk in a pan and bring gently to the boil, lower the heat and simmer for 30 minutes. Strain and add the honey, mix well. The mixture does not keep for more than a couple of days.

for several hours and then, as with a coffee percolator, liquid was filtered through it very slowly. The process was repeated to achieve the correct volume of liquid in ratio to the weight of active ingredient.

Soaking, or maceration, was also a straightforward procedure. The active ingredient was infused in liquid, often alcohol, at room temperature, for a set period of time (generally around seven days), and regularly shaken. The liquid was then strained and filtered. Oils were squeezed out of plants or seeds with a tincture press. As tinctures are concentrates, a dose was measured in drops. These could be combined with other mixtures or sold as a sole treatment.

EMULSIONS

In making medicines, the chemist used his skills to combine the correct weight of active ingredients in an appropriate liquid base (most commonly water), with colouring and flavouring, to produce a palatably flavoured mixture. Emulsions were more complex to make; these combine two liquid substances that would not normally mix. Emulsions should not separate in the way that vinaigrette (an unstable emulsion) does. The science requires that the tension between two liquids should be lowered, using an emulsifying agent, so that the small particles of one liquid can be suspended in the other. Victorian pharmacists used emulsifiers such as egg yolk, soap and gum.

ELIXIRS

Medicine could be flavoured to make it more palatable. This was known as an elixir; it could be mixed into a syrupy solution with sugar or honey to produce a soothing linctus for the treatment of coughs, and the active ingredient might even be mixed in a base of sherry or wine. Not all liquid medicine was taken orally; the chemist could be asked to produce ear drops, sprays for the nose or throat, eye drops or gargles.

FINISHING TOUCHES

As medicine began to be sold in multi-doses, chemists used ridged bottles to indicate doses and sold glass or porcelain measuring spoons. Some mixtures could not be mixed, because together they would combine to give off gas and become unstable. They were sold in separate bottles and the patient was instructed to combine them in a single dose before consuming. The enterprising chemist had special glass bottles produced that bore his name. Up until the 1930s, these were sealed with corks; the chemist used a cork press, which squeezed the tip of the cork to persuade it to fit into the neck of the bottle.

Even then he was not finished, for presentation was all important, no matter how efficacious the mixture. A label was put onto the top of the cork and this was then be covered with a fluted paper cap, while the neck of the bottle was wrapped in white paper.

OINTMENTS, CREAMS AND LINIMENTS

Ointments and creams have been used for thousands of years to help soothe and heal the skin. *King's Grace's oyntement* was created for Henry VIII 'to coole and dry and comfort the Member', an indication that he suffered for at least one of his many sexual dalliances. To make an ointment, the chemist mixed the prescribed active ingredients, with a small amount of a greasy base such as petroleum jelly, goose grease, lard or lanolin. These were combined on an ointment slab or in a pestle and mortar and, when the preparation was perfectly smooth, the remainder of the base could be mixed in.

Recipes

Horseradish Syrup

For a persistent cough, adults can take two teaspoons three times a day.

Chopped horseradish root 1½ oz

*Golden granulated sugar 1 lb
(or a jar of honey)*

Put the chopped horseradish root in a pan with 1½ pints of water and bring gently to the boil. Reduce the heat and simmer gently for 30 minutes. Remove from the heat and set aside to cool. Strain the liquid and discard the root, return the liquid to the heat and simmer until reduced to 7 fl oz. Add the sugar or the honey and allow to dissolve slowly, then simmer gently, stirring continuously until the sweetener has completely dissolved.

Ointment could be stored in jars, but was often put into lead tubes for ease of use. Filling these was a skill the chemist had to develop. New tubes were purchased, and these were open at their base. The chemist removed the cap of the tube, put his ointment into a roll of paper, placed one end of the roll of paper into the base of the tube and applied pressure to the other end of the roll, forcing the ointment from the paper into the tube. When the tube was almost full, its end was turned over, a little at a time, until ointment began to squeeze out of the open nozzle. The cap was replaced and a label stuck into position.

Creams were made using the same principal ingredients, but with a slightly different method. The greasy base and an emulsifying agent were heated with water, and then the active ingredient was added. This method produced a smoother, less greasy product that blended into the skin. A label in the Boots archive for Smith's Cremola promised:

> *This product is unequalled for softening and beautifying the Skin, and from defending it from the influence of summer sun. Directions – A little to be applied to the Skin and rubbed in until quite dry. The most delicate needlework may be undertaken without washing the hands after using it.*

Health and safety was less of a concern, but some of these concoctions were lethal. *The Chemist & Druggist* of 15 February 1868 reported a fatal accident from the ignition of a liniment in Liverpool. The story explained that an old man, Peter Bragan, obtained a colourless liniment for his rheumatism. He gave this to his wife and asked her to rub it on one of his hips. She poured some of the liquid on her hands and after rubbing her husband for some time, in order to increase its efficacy, she warmed her hands at the fire. The liquid on her hands ignited and she was severely burned. Her husband approached to render assistance and the liquid on his hip ignited. His clothes were burned and he sustained such serious injuries that he died in the Northern Hospital a few days after the accident.

PLASTERS AND POULTICES

Plasters were a popular method of delivering medicine to the skin, not an early version of the Band-Aid. Making them was an incredibly sticky and painstaking business, but they were very popular with the customers. Robert Wood Johnson (1845–1910), one of the three brothers who started Johnson & Johnson, began his career as an apprentice to an apothecary in Poughkeepsie, New York, in order to avoid being drafted into the Civil War. Making plasters was his least favourite job: 'probably no other branch of the pharmaceutical art has been the occasion of so much toil, anxiety and failure and discouragement before any measure of success was met.' (Quoted by Lawrence G. Foster, *Robert Wood Johnson: The Gentleman Rebel.*)

Having been out of favour for some years, the system is now used to deliver hormone replacement therapy (HRT) or nicotine to the skin via what we call patches. In Victorian times, they were used to relieve aches and pains: mustard plasters heated up painful areas; capsicum plasters were used to relieve muscle pain; and irritants caused blistering of the skin.

To make a plaster, the pharmacist first gently heated a plaster mix, consisting of the active ingredient mixed with a sticky substance such as beeswax, lanolin or resin until it was a spreadable consistency. A piece of chamois leather, or calico fabric, was stretched over a board to form the back of the plaster. A plaster stencil was selected; these were available in various shapes to fit the breast, shoulder, back, ear and so on, and a copy of this was made on white paper. This paper stencil was dampened, and then the warm plaster mix was spread evenly over it. The stencil was then applied to the fabric or cloth back, and when the plaster was almost dry the paper was peeled off. The plaster shape was then cut out, leaving a small border all the way around. When dry, the plasters were stored in boxes, with each one separated from the other with a sheet of greaseproof paper. If, when applied, the warmth of the skin was not sufficient to allow the plaster to adhere, the patient was advised to warm it gently and try again.

Poultices were designed to soothe, calm, and ease soreness and inflammation by applying a substance directly onto the skin. The plant or herb was mashed to release its active ingredients, then mixed with boiling water and applied as hot as was comfortable. The vinegar and brown paper referred to in the nursery rhyme about Jack and Jill would have been a traditional poultice designed to bring Jack's bruise to the surface of the skin and reduce swelling. Poultices are messy, but were tremendously popular.

Often, young men suffered terribly from boils on the back of their necks, the unhappy combination of hormones and stiff starched collars. A common treatment was to pour boiling water into a glass milk bottle, then empty the water out and quickly place the steaming bottle over the boil. As the bottle cools, a vacuum is created and the pus is drawn out of the boil – it was said to be horribly painful. A poultice was then applied to draw out the rest of the ooze.

PESSARIES, SUPPOSITORIES AND BOUGIES

Specific medical treatments were developed for the various body cavities. All used the same basic method of preparation, although each item was of a different shape. Suppositories, shaped like bullets, treated problems in the anal passage; haemorrhoids and constipation caused discomfort then, as now. Pessaries, also bullet shaped but slightly larger in size, were designed to treat vaginal infections. The unfamiliar bougie – long, thin and tapering – was used to treat the urethra, bladder, prostate and the nose. Chemists also made suppositories and pessaries for cows and horses, and had especially large moulds to suit.

Recipes

Bread Poultice

Apply directly over a splinter to draw the fragment to the surface.

Soak two pieces of bread in hot water or hot milk; strain and apply the poultice to the affected area, keeping it in place with a piece of gauze or muslin for 15–30 minutes.

Mustard Poultice

For the relief of congestion or coughs and discomfort in the chest.

Mix ½ teaspoon of mustard seed powder with 1 tablespoon of flour. Slowly add hot water until a paste has formed. Spread on half of a piece of muslin or flannel, fold over the material so the paste does not touch the skin and apply to the chest or back for 15–30 minutes.

The active ingredients are contained in a base designed to melt at body temperature. Cocoa butter and a glycerine-gelatine mixture were commonly used as a base in the nineteenth century. These ingredients were heated slowly and gently in pan with a spout over a water bath. A little of this solution was mixed on a tile with the active ingredient. When this was absorbed, it was mixed thoroughly with the rest of the base. The moulds were made of stainless steel and brass, which were lubricated with oil or a soap solution and then the mixture was poured in. The two halves of the bougie mould were screwed together after they were filled, to force out excess. The following example is taken from *Pharmaceutical Formulas*:

Nutritive Suppository

Dry beef peptone in powder ℨvj.
Cocoa-butter ℥j.

Shred the cocoa-butter and melt it by the heat of a water-bath, triturate the peptone in a warm mortar with about half of the melted fat, return to the dish in portions, stirring all the time, and when the whole is thoroughly mixed pour into I-dr. moulds (iced).

ENEMAS

Enemas, or clysters, have been in use as long as man has been obsessed by bowel movements, namely since ancient times. In the nineteenth century, they were considered an efficient method of clearing the bowels. It was normal practice, particularly among the well-to-do, to administer enemas. The inventive Victorians created all manner of fancy apparatus for ease of use.

TOILETRIES

Victorian ladies liked to preserve an image of fragile femininity. Preserving the complexion was acceptable, but wearing visible make-up was frowned upon. Beatrix Potter (1866–1943) observed of an actress in 1883: 'Miss Ellen Terry's complexion is made of such expensive enamel that she can only afford to wash her face once a fortnight and removes smuts in the meantime with a wet sponge.' The selection of available make-up was very limited – a note scribbled on a scrap of paper and despatched to Mr Llewellyn, the chemist, was preserved, and reads: '1 lip stick the cheapest you got. Red.'

A little powder or lip salve was acceptable as long as there were no hint of artifice. Cold creams were well regarded, however, since they were, as *Pharmaceutical Formulas* put it, 'one of the ungents of antiquity'. Protecting the skin from the sun was important, and freckles were regarded as an unpardonable blemish – pity the poor red heads.

☠ *Rose Freckle Lotion* ☠

Zinci sulphocarbol ʒss.
Glycerini ʒss.
Spt. Rectificat ʒj.
Tr. cocci ʒss
Aq. flor. aurantii ʒij.
Aq. rosae ad. ʒviij.

In 1891, Helena Rubenstein (1870–1965) launched her first skin cream in Australia, Valaze, using lanolin, the by-product of sheep farming. She opened a beauty salon in London in 1902, just a year after Queen Victoria's death.

To promote beauty products, actresses, then as now, led the way. Ellen Terry (1847–1928) was the face of Rimmel cosmetics and Lillie Langtry (1853–1929) appeared in an advertisement for Pears soap. Peter McEwan, author of *Pharmaceutical Formulas* (1898), maintains that toilet requisites are as important as any class of goods retailed by chemists and druggists: 'they appeal to the tastes of the refined and the rich – to the beautiful and those who wish to be – and they afford the retailer splendid opportunity for exhibition of skill in compounding and taste in packing.' These were products that the chemist supplied, often on request, for the toiletries and cosmetics business

was in its infancy. Many recipes were exchanged in *The Chemist & Druggist*. Interestingly, McEwan also despairs of the stupidity of the customer:

> *the public expect too much from the class of specialities called 'beautifiers'. It frequently happens that the higher priced an article is, and the more highly it is vaunted, the better its success. This applied particularly to the class of articles we are now dealing with, and is a source of danger to the compounder's self-respect.*

HAIR REMOVAL

It is perhaps surprising to learn that Victorian ladies – shrouded as they were from top to toe – were still obsessed with hair removal. The products on offer were heavy-duty, as *The Chemist & Druggist* observed:

> *These require caution, as they are apt to injure the skin. We have omitted those which contain yellow sulphide of arsenic (orpiment) as there is danger of it being absorbed and the object can be accomplished without its use. The powders require to be kept in well closed bottles or boxes, and no more should be mixed with liquid than is required to be used at once.*

☜ James Crossley began selling his Eno's Fruit Salts from his pharmacy in Newcastle-upon-Tyne in the 1850's. By the end of the century it was sold all over the world.

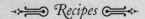

Recipes

German Lip Salve

To soothe and moisturise dry, chapped lips.

———————

Butter of cacao ½ oz
Oil of almonds ½ oz
Essence of lemon 6 drops

Melt the cacao butter and almond oil over a gentle heat, then stir in the essence of lemon.

Cheap Pomade

Use to style hair, leaving it thick and shiny.

———————

Lard 1 lb
Palm oil 1½ oz
Oil of citronella 20 drops
Oil of bergamot 10 drops
Oil of lemon 10 drops
Oil of cassia 5 drops

Melt the lard and palm oil, strain and when cooled somewhat add the perfume.

Men, too, were eager customers, looking for hair oils or pomades to keep their hair sleek and shiny. Hair dyes were frowned upon, but they existed nonetheless. Men looked for the means of darkening greying whiskers and moustaches and both sexes wanted to hide white hair, though most people were too nervous to try. Women were deemed to be fast if they coloured their hair; men could be a little bolder.

In *The Druggist's General Receipt Book*, Henry Beasley advises his readers: 'It may be well to remind our readers that all medical authorities strongly condemn the use of lead in hair dyes.' Curiously, he then details a recipe for Mercurial Black Dye: 'A weak solution of perchloride of mercury, used for some days, followed by a wash containing hyposulphite of soda; *not without danger.*' This recipe is taken from Henry Beasley's *The Druggist's General Receipt Book*:

☠ *Black Pomatum, in sticks, for the eyebrows, whiskers etc* ☠

Prepared lard melted with a third of its weight of wax in winter, or half in summer, is coloured with levigated ivory-black and strained through tammy, or any material which will permit the fine particles of ivory-black to pass through.

    Stir it constantly and when it begins to thicken pour it into paper moulds.

Bay rum was one of the most popular hair preparations – it is still sold today. McEwan observes:

…its use in England is confined to the well-to-do, it is otherwise in the New World, especially in the United States. There it is used by middle-class and first-class hairdressers with much liberality as a wash for the skin after shaving and as a cooling application to the head. The comparatively low U.S. spirit duty doubtless accounts for this liberality, just as the high British spirit duty prevents its greater use.

An advertisement from 1880 shows the range of products available to the pharmacist from the gloriously named wholesale and export druggist R. H. Millard, Son & Appleton.

PERFUMES

If certain cosmetic toilet preparations were frowned upon, perfumes were not. Exuding a delicate fragrance was the very essence of Victorian femininity and light floral perfumes were favoured. The wealthy could afford French perfumes; Sarah

---

Recipes

Floral Perfume

A delicate fragrance, which can be made up using many combinations of herbs to suit your personal taste.

Add five drops each of rose, jasmine and lavender oils to 2 oz fragrance-free moisturiser or avocado oil. If you can't find rose oil, or it's too expensive, try rose geranium oil. A few drops of musk can be added for a richer perfume.

A Light, Summer Perfume

A light scent for the warmer days of the year.

Add a few drops of lemon verbena, lemongrass, and rose geranium oils to 2 oz of white wine. Shake well before using. For a different scent, try adding the oils to a fruit brandy.

Bernhardt (1844–1923) was known to favour *Jicky* by Guerlain. The French perfumier Eugene Rimmel (1820–1887) opened the House of Rimmel in 1834, and was awarded a Royal warrant by Queen Victoria. Assisted by his sons, he created an innovative product range including mouthwashes, toilet vinegar (a light fragrance supposedly like Eau de Cologne), scented steam vaporisers and fragranced pomades. Rimmel offered ladies the following advice in *The Book of Perfumes*, published in 1865:

> *Use simple extracts of flowers, which can never hurt you, in preference to compounds, which generally contain musk and other ingredients likely to affect the head. Above all, avoid strong coarse perfumes: and remember, that if a woman's temper may be told from her handwriting, her good taste and good breeding may as easily be ascertained by the perfume she uses. Whilst a lady charms with the delicate ethereal fragrance she sheds around her, aspiring vulgarity will betray itself by a mouchoir [handkerchief] redolent of common perfumes.*

Chemists were very happy to make up their own perfumes, products on which they could often make a reasonable profit. The industry trade magazine, *The Chemist & Druggist*, was packed with recipes. Many fragrances were named after members of the Royal Family: Mary Stuart Bouquet, Eugenia Bouquet, Princess Beatrice Bouquet. Others were named after places: Brighton Nosegay, Folkestone Bouquet, Midland Counties Bouquet. One recipe was deliberately nameless and was devised so that the chemist could make a perfume 'Bouquet of X' and fill in the name of his home town to appeal to local customers and visitors. Perfumed waters – or handkerchief waters – were popular, as was Eau de Cologne. 'Jockey Club' was a very popular blend, though the name hardly suggests a delicate fragrance.

Chemists were also called upon to perfume theatres or ballrooms. Sometimes an atomiser was used to spray the entrances half an hour before the public were due to arrive, as well as the seats where they would sit. Even programmes were perfumed, by keeping them in boxes between sheets of perfumed paper. Ballrooms were scented by using a floor polish perfumed with lavender oil.

Perfumes extended across a range of products. Chemists made knobs of perfume from 'Spanish Paste', which could be dropped into writing cases, jewellery or glove boxes to keep the contents smelling fresh. Ribbons or skins of leather were perfumed, the former to offer that subtle fragrance, the latter with a view to using them to line boxes.

The Victorians, it seems, were not so very different, obsessing about the same physical failings that bother us today: body hair, pimples, baldness, hair colour. *Plus ça change.*

Recipes

Eau de Cologne No 1

A truly elegant scent.

———

Oil of bergamot 60 drops
Oil of lemon 60 drops
Oil of rosemary 60 drops
Oil of lavender 30 drops
Oil of neroli 38 drops
Oil of citronella 8 drops
Rectified spirit (such as vodka) 16 oz
Orange flower water 4 oz

Mix oils with the rectified spirit, gradually add the orange flower water, then filter.

CHAPTER 6

2000 ITEMS IN STOCK

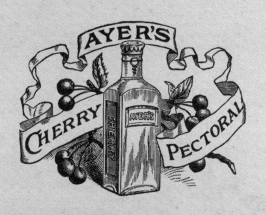

'Water, air and cleanness are the chief articles in my pharmacy.'

NAPOLEON BONAPARTE

*J*esse Boot realised early in his career that customers coming into the shop to purchase their medicines were quite prepared to be sold many other items as well. Although drugs were the primary business, toiletries and new lines were designed to act as an advertisement for pharmacy and patent medicines. So anything that maintained the essential link with health and beauty, was acceptable: scouring drops, baby bottles, indelible ink, boot black, bed pans, curry powder, gun powder, furniture polish, enema syringes, Harrisons' Cleansing Drink for Cows and any number of patent medicines.

Nor was Boot alone in his practice. Pharmacists would buy in all manner of exotic items and hunt down recipes so that they could supply just about anything else required, from sherbet to fireworks. Boot himself began to sell Christmas cards at the end of the nineteenth century. He had his quirks, though: he stocked tooth powders and pastes, but refused to sell toothbrushes.

The entrepreneurial Jesse Boot was always ready to experiment with new lines. In Goosegate, the first Boots in the centre of Nottingham, an ironmongers' department was opened in the basement. This was a real departure for Boot because it was the first time he sold goods that had no link with health or medicine. The department was not a success and closed within a couple of years.

BOOT'S BOOKLOVER'S LIBRARY

Jesse's wife Florence, who had also been brought up in the retail trade, wanted to put her expertise in the sales of stationery, artists materials, books and gifts to good use. Unlike the ironmongery, her venture was a roaring success.

The Goosegate area was largely working class, but standards of living were rising and rates of literacy improving. Attendance at school became mandatory for children under the age of 10 in 1880. The shop was surrounded by chapels, and the sales of bibles in particular were strong. In 1898, the book departments were turned into Boot's Booklover's Library: customers were charged 2d to borrow a book, and the concept was hugely popular. The books were always kept at the back of the store so customers had to walk right through to get to them. It also gave people something to do while they waited for their prescriptions. At its height in 1938, the department was attracting one million subscribers, with books being exchanged at a rate of 35 million per year. The libraries were closed in 1966.

BOVRIL, CUSTARD AND WORCESTERSHIRE SAUCE

The sales of foodstuffs seemed a natural progression: why not sell healthy food products? Experimental chemists were at the forefront of developments in food processing, devising ingenious chemical solutions that ensured the preservation of foods and introducing spicy flavours to stimulate the palette and bland food for delicate constitutions. Indeed, it could be argued that it was chemists who created the first convenience foods.

Boot's errand boy G.R. Elliott recalls the sale of a new line (tinned salmon) causing a sensation:

> *The usual price at that time was 8d; Mr Boot's price was 4½d a tin. Good quality, too. After the news circulated, the sale was sensational. A case contained 3 dozen tins and we sold as many as 40 cases on a Saturday. 120 dozen tins in a single day from one shop. Hard to believe, is it not? Many of the orders were 'a tin of salmon, please, and will you open it?' Tin openers were not to be found in every poor house then.*

Beef tea, which is always dished up in Victorian novels at the first hint of weakness, was a regular feature of chemist's recipe books. Johnston's Fluid Beef, better known as Bovril, was created in 1870 by John Lawson Johnston

(1839–1900). He was commissioned to supply nutritious food to the troops of Napoleon III (1808–1873), then engaged in a dispute with Prussia. Johnston could not find enough beef to fulfil the order and came up with the idea of a meaty concentrate. In 1855, Queen Victoria required Fortnum & Mason to 'dispatch without delay to Miss Nightingale in Scutari a concentrated beef tea.' Boots started selling a Fluid Beef product in 1900, which offered 'a sustaining drink in a minute'. It was designed for invalids, athletes and tourists.

Alfred Bird (1811–1878) was a qualified chemist and druggist and registered pharmacist with a thriving business. His wife, Elizabeth, was unable to digest any dishes prepared with eggs or bread and containing yeast, so he set to work to create a product that would make her life easier. After six years of work, he produced his first concoction, Bird's Fermenting Powder, which produced bread and cakes with a light consistency. These were used in the Crimean War to enable the troops to have fresh bread, instead of hard-tack biscuits, as it was not possible to store live yeast.

However, it was not the Fermenting Powder that ensured Bird's name is still a familiar one today. Mrs Bird was very partial to custard but, being made from eggs and cream, this upset her delicate digestion. Her doting husband turned his attention to the production of eggless custard. He used the thickening properties of cornflour to produce Bird's Custard Powder, first formulated in 1837. Both products were sold from Bird's chemist outlet and were quickly put into commercial production.

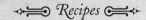

Recipes

Browning Sauce

Add a few drops to sauces, soups, gravies and stews for extra colour and flavour.

Granulated sugar 32 oz
Water 32 oz
Indian soy 16 oz
Walnut ketchup 3 oz
Mushroom ketchup 3 oz

Combine all the ingredients in a pan over a high heat, stirring well. When thoroughly mixed, allow to cool and bottle for use.

Legend has it that John Lea (1791–1874), a pharmacist in Worcester, and his assistant William Perrins (1793–1867) created their famous Worcestershire Sauce after a passing Maharajah asked if they stocked any spicy condiments. It was first produced commercially in 1837 and was immediately a roaring success. Good marketing helped: Mr Lea and Mr Perrin persuaded ocean liners to promote their sauce. Waiters were paid to offer it to passengers, who would develop a taste for it and then purchase bottles to take home with them. Lea and Perrin did not want to encourage imitators and the recipe was a closely guarded secret. The original recipe was uncovered by an archivist, Mr Brian Keogh in the early 1980s. He unearthed notes from a skip, dating from the mid-1800s, that list both the ingredients and quantities: soy sauce, fish, cloves, lemons, pickles and peppers. So successful was the sauce that the partners gave up on the pharmacy side of their business.

☠ *Blancmange Powder* ☠

Best cornflour lb. j.
Sago flour lb. j.
Oil of lemon ♏ x.
Oil of nutmeg ♏ v.
Oil of cassia ♏ iij.

Mix the oils with an ounce of the sago, gradually add the rest of the powders, and sift twice. The powder may also be flavoured with essence of ratafia instead of the above. Mix it up into 1½ oz packets.

Directions. – Make the contents of this packet into a smooth paste with half a cupful of milk. Dissolve 2 oz of caster-sugar in a pint of milk and add it, whilst boiling, to the paste stirring. Transfer to a saucepan, boil for five minutes, and pour into a mould.

TONICS AND DRINKS

Carbonated waters had become popular late in the eighteenth century. It was American pharmacists who began adding fruit extracts and herbs such as dandelion and sarsaparilla to make the first flavoured carbonated soft drinks. Dr John Pemberton (1831–1888), a pharmacist from Atlanta Georgia, invented Coca Cola in 1886, and it was sold at his pharmacy's soda fountain. The magic mix was sold as syrup, which was mixed with carbonated water at the soda fountain. First sold in Britain in 1900 and marketed as a tonic until 1905, it originally contained extracts of cocaine. The following recipe for Dandelion and Burdock is taken from a collection in a diary dated 1899, in the Boots archive:

☠ *Dandelion & Burdock* ☠
– to make 6 gallons

2 bottles Jessops herb beer extract
2lbs of sugar
2 oz yeast
2 pints Dandelion and Burdock syrup
Add 2 galls of boiling water to the sugar and extract.

Then add 4 galls of cold water, it would be better to warm a little out of the 4 galls, on purpose, to make it ferment. Now add the yeast and let it stand all night covered. In the morning take off the yeast and add the dandelion and burdock syrup.

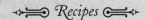

Milk Lemonade

A refreshing family drink.

———•◆•———

Dissolve 1½ lbs of sugar in a quart of boiling water, add half a pint of fresh lemon juice and the same of sherry; and, lastly, two-thirds of a pint of cold milk. Stir together and strain.

Stir it and then put in a barrel with about four tablespoons of Jessops Fluff.

Pharmacists in the United Kingdom were not slow to spot the potential of these new drinks and quickly purchased the apparatus necessary to make their own mineral waters. The trade magazine *The Chemist & Druggist* devoted much editorial space to the 'apparatus and materials used in making Aerated Waters'. This excerpt, from the issue dated 15 February 1868, is enthusiastic:

...these machines which vary in price from £50 upwards, are made with Marble Enveloping Box and contain Cans for syrups, and an ingenious machine for reducing the ice to snow, and forming an Ice Cream. The beverage is very popular in the United States, and must we think become so here and on the continent. These machines were exhibited at the Paris Exhibition of 1867, and nothing in the portable line met with such success as the Ice Cream Soda Water, or Soda Americain.

Chemists were advised to visit factories when purchasing, so as to see the apparatus actually in operation.

The water was sold in a siphon and the siphon bottle was returnable. Some chemists found bottles were not coming back to them, so they made a charge of two shillings on every siphon, to be refunded when the bottle was returned. This expense deterred many customers, so other chemists advocated the use of labels for regular customers, clearly stating name and address, and the date the siphon was taken and the date for it to be returned.

The Chemist & Druggist offered many recipes for soluble essences to mix with tonic water to provide a refreshing drink – and promised that these 'should not present much difficulty to any chemist who has at his disposal a series of artificial fruit essences, essential oils, tinctures and French Bouquets.'

Any businesslike pharmacist would have labels printed up to use on their own range of products. ☞

The magazine reminded its readers to 'keep the *fruit* always prominent and the *flower* subsidiary, as few palettes can appreciate the taste of scents.' One such recipe for Lemon-Squash Essence, see below, contains a startling ingredient:

☠ *Lemon-squash Essence* ☠

Sol. Essence of Lemon (No 1) ℥x.
Oil of bergamot ʒj.
Asbestos, in shreds ʒj.
Shake together and filter

Lemon Kali was a hugely popular drink. The dried ingredients, tartaric acid and bicarbonate of soda were mixed and then placed on paper. A little of the sugar was put in a mortar, the oil of lemon sprinkled over and mixed well through. The remaining sugar was added gradually, until well blended. This was then mixed with the soda and the acid and sifted several times:

☠ *Lemon Kali* ☠

Pulv. Sacch. Alb. lb. iv.
Pulv. Acid tart. lb. ij.
Pulv sodæ bicarb lb ij.
Ol. Limones ʒij.

Ginger Beer powder was much the same recipe, with the quantity of lemon oil reduced and the addition of ginger essential oil. In *Pharmaceutical Formulas*, a collection of recipes taken from the trade magazine *The Chemist & Druggist*, the editor Peter McEwan observes: 'It must be confessed that American drinks are as far ahead of English as a glass of Laurent-Perrier champagne is above a glass of the gooseberry article, and it might be profitable to take a lesson or two from the transatlantic experience.'

Chemists brewed root beer, herbal beer, lemonade and ginger beer to sell.

As well as making the beverage from scratch themselves, they could cheat and purchase bottles of ready-made Herb Beer Extract. These were added to boiling water, the yeast popped in, and the resulting drink would be ready for bottling and consumption in just a day or two.

Essences of wine, such as cherry wine or orange wine, could also be prepared and sold. After 1893, however, chemists were prohibited from making and selling any essence that contained more than three per cent of proof spirit without a licence. Chemists were mollified only when the Board of Inland Revenue tempered the original notice and promised that it 'would not interfere with the manufacture and sale of ginger wine or raspberry-wine essences without licence when intended for temperance and summer beverages.'

Chemists experienced similar problems in selling 'medicinal' wines. This was permissible only if the drink contained specific proportions of an active ingredient – and if it tasted bad, this was a bonus as far as the authorities were concerned. An invalid might be advised to take quinine wine, coka wine, beef and iron wine or, worryingly, senna wine. Curiously, despite strictures on alcohol sales, *The Chemist & Druggist* supplied its readers with recipes enabling them to produce a positive cocktail cabinet of bitters and liqueurs: Wormwood bitters, Benedictine, Chartreuse and even Absinthe from a combination of essential oils and the appropriate spirit.

Recipes

Lemon Verbena tea

Take one cup three times a day as a calmative.

Water 1 pint

Fresh lemon verbena leaves or flowers 1 oz (use half measures if using dried)

Bring the water to the boil in a pan. Remove from the heat and add the leaves or flowers and leave to infuse for five minutes. Strain and discard the lemon verbena before drinking.

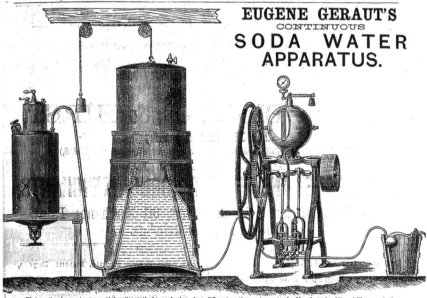

EUGENE GERAUT'S
CONTINUOUS
SODA WATER
APPARATUS.

We have the pleasure to give you below the particulars and prices of our different continuous Apparatus for Manufacturing Mineral Waters and other gaseous beverages.

Having given this branch of our business our especial study and attention, we can warrant our Apparatus with perfect confidence, and we trust that the guarantee we offer as to their proper construction and adaptation, added to the moderation of our prices, will ensure us the preference of your orders; and should you kindly favour us with your patronage, we promise, on our part, to do at all times our utmost to deserve your confidence.

Owing to the great and important improvements we have made in this Apparatus, we can say that it combines every advantage with regard to solidity, strength, and compactness; all the pieces are mechanically joined together, and may be separated with the greatest facility.

This Apparatus, by its superior advantages, may be said to defy all competition; it is not, however, our intention here to criticise in detail the Apparatus of our competitors, leaving that matter to more able critics; we would not attempt to raise ourselves in public opinion by depreciating others; we would simply say to all who may favour us by their preference that the experience we have acquired in the manufacture of Machines for Mineral Waters, united to our mechanical system, enables us to offer on lower terms the advantages of a superior Apparatus.

PARTS OF THE APPARATUS.	PRICES.
A Machine with one or two Pumps. Very powerful Condenser, ten times larger, and tenfold greater power than any yet made in the United Kingdom. Manometer with Dial. Very sensitive Safety Valve. Water Gauge, which indicates the quantity of water there is always in the Condenser. Leaden Generator, with horizontal Fan and acid holder, which gives the advantage of great economy of acid. Gasometer.	No. 1. Continuous principle, single action, condenser, holding about 8 gallons, complete, to make 4,000 bottles per day, ready to be worked by hand or steam, £50 nett. No. 2. Continuous principle, double action, 12 gallons, complete, to make 8,000 bottles per day, £70 nett. No. 3. Double action, to make 12,000 bottles per day, complete, £120 nett. Corking and Bottling Machine, £7 10s. nett. Syphon Filler, £4 10s. nett.

N.B.—Nipples are made for filling bottles if required.

SELTZOGENES,

For the Preparation of Seltzer Water, Eau de Vichy, Soda Water, Sparkling Lemonade, Aerated Wines, &c.

This SELTZOGENE differs materially from the numerous kinds that have been from time to time introduced. It is made without any joint, and entirely of one piece of glass, effecting two most essential advantages, viz., of rendering the apparatus quite free from leakage and preserving the aerated water, &c., any length of time in the highest state of perfection. In this apparatus the aerated liquids are guaranteed to *improve by keeping,* not only as regards strength, but in *freshness and purity*—a result hitherto unaccomplished.

WHOLESALE AS FOLLOWS :—2-pint, wire, 13s. ; cane-covered, 13s. 6d. ; 5-pint, wire, 18s. ; cane covered, 19s. Strongly silver-plated, 5s. each extra. 3-pint size, with richly-ornamented Stand, and strongly silver-plated, 27s.

Powders for the above, 2-pint, 20s. ; 3-pint, 22s. ; 5-pint, 36s. per dozen boxes.

SYPHONS.

These we make in various sizes of thick, strong glass, **and guarantee the mountings to be exclusively of the purest and finest English block tin,** and so applied that if by accident the glass should get broken, new ones can be refitted at a trifling cost, without the Syphon being returned to us. 1,500 a day can easily be filled by one person without previous experience.

We have taken every possible care in the manufacture, and can say with confidence that for finish and perfection of workmanship there has nothing like it been yet introduced in the United Kingdom.

WHOLESALE PRICES.—Large size, clear or blue glass, holding 1½ pint, £18 per gross ; small size, clear or blue glass, holding about 1 pint, £16 16s. per gross.

Messrs. E. GERAUT & CO. beg to inform the Trade that they decline to repair any Apparatus except their own make.

E. GERAUT & CO.,
Sole Manufacturers in the United Kingdom of the PATENT IMPROVED SELTZOGENES, SYPHONS, &c.,
1 CORPORATION BUILDINGS, FARRINGDON ROAD, E.C.

An advertisement from Chemist & Druggist Diary *shows assorted apparatus for making soda water. In the latter part of the century, pharmacists made syrups to flavour the soda water thus enhancing the thrill.*

EQUIPMENT AND ACCESSORIES

It must have been of considerable relief to the chemist that there was some stock he didn't have to make from scratch. There was a brisk trade in items that might be required for both the nursery and the sick room, precisely the kind of item we still look for in the chemists today. Pewter feeding bottles were in use throughout the nineteenth century, but chemists stocked newer designs made from cream earthenware, blue and white china, or glass bottles. Many of these were flattened ovals, with a hole on the upper side through which the bottle was filled; a piece of cloth or chamois leather created a nipple of sorts for the infant to suck at one end. Preserved cows teats were also used as nipples, and were tied on to the bottle with a piece of string. Vulcanised rubber was not invented until the 1840s and the early teats smelled dreadful.

Self-feeding devices were created. A length of tube led from the bottle to a bone mouth shield and a teat so that the baby could be fed unattended. The downside was that the design was impossible to clean efficiently and caused infections. They were dubbed 'killer bottles' for good reason. The banana shaped bottle, with wide openings at each end, was much easier to clean but did not make an appearance until the mid-1880s.

If the mother was suffering from sore nipples, she could use perforated shields of glass, pewter, ivory or silver, and use breast pumps to express her milk. Pap boats or cups were a popular style of infant feeder. Some desperate mothers would sell their breast milk while their own infants were fed from a pap boat on

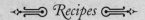

Tomato Sauce

A flavoursome condiment to accompany dishes of your choice.

Ripe tomatoes 6
Small pinch of ground mace
Salt ½ oz
Sugar 1 oz
A couple of cloves
Cayenne as desired
Shallots 2
Vinegar 5 oz

Cut the tomatoes into small pieces and soak with the other ingredients in vinegar until they are quite tender. Next, beat this mixture to a pulp in a mortar and press through a sieve. Heat the liquid until it boils and leave for a few minutes. Bottle whilst hot.

pap – a combination of boiled water and flour with perhaps a little bread or egg added to it. The design of a pap boat resembled the plastic invalid feeding cups used in hospitals today: a covered bowl with a handle and a long spout through which the baby could feed. These were made from china or silver and were also used in the sick room. Food warmers – hollow pedestals which held oil and a wick – allowed the pap to be warmed and were fully used in both the nursery and sick room.

For the invalid, there was a selection of equipment to ease their lives. Sputum mugs and bottles allowed patients to spit out phlegm into pretty decorated containers that concealed their fetid contents; these were also fiendishly difficult to clean. Inevitably there were also many designs of bed warmers and bed pans.

Patients suffering from chest complaints had little medication to ease their discomfort. Steam inhalations were considered beneficial. Bronchitis kettles, with very long spouts, were purpose-built for the job. The kettle was placed on the fire to produce a steady supply of steam, whilst the patient sat under a cloth, enjoying the benefit of the steam but, crucially, at a safe distance from the fire.

The Nelson Inhaler was a rounded glass or ceramic bottle. Directions for use state:

> *For the inhalation of the vapours of Hot Water the water should be boiling and the container not more than half filled. When infusions are required the ingredients should be placed in the inhaler and Boiling Water poured upon them. Volatile and other ingredients should be added to the Boiling Water.*

Enema syringes, designed to introduce medication or liquids into the body, via the rectum, were widely used until the mid-1850s. Many colourful devices allowed for the self-administration of such a treatment. In essence, the patient sat on an upright nozzle and the medication was delivered – with powerful force – when the piston was depressed. Makes your eyes water just to

Soda Water & Ginger Beer.

An illustration from around 1830 shows customers enjoing the heady experience of soda water and ginger beer in a London pharmacist's shop.

think about it. There was no subtlety to the process and the devices were blamed for causing numerous injuries. A new innovation around the 1860s was to include a long tube attachment so that the device could also be used in the vagina as a contraceptive douche.

Medicine chests were in demand from the more affluent customers. Victorian gentlemen and women were enthusiastic travellers and felt vulnerable without medical supplies and hard drugs close to hand. Chests contained a formula book, weights and measures, a pestle and mortar, a lancet, blistering plasters and leech tubes – a basic DIY pharmacy kit.

Previous page: Chest complaints were very common and bronchitis kettles used the therapeutic effects of aromatic steam to relieve bronchial congestion.

Essential drugs included opium for pain relief, usually in the form of laudanum or tincture of opium; ipecacuanha as an expectorant and emetic; turkey rhubarb as a digestive tonic or purgative; and Dr James' Fever Powder for fevers.

HEARING AIDS AND A CURE FOR DEAFNESS

Hearing devices were found in the pharmacy. The chemist could supply trumpet headbands, perhaps teamed with a bone acoustic fan, designed to transmit sound, or alternatively an air acoustic fan, which was held behind the ear in the same manner as a cupped hand. A.C. Grønbeck , a Danish ear nose and throat physician, observed in 1891:

> *Most hearing aids are of such a size and shape that they clearly draw attention to the imperfection of the wearer. This condition is, as we have experienced, enough to make many people shrink back from using such an aid.*

If all else failed, a herbal medicine promised a solution taken from *The Working Man's Model Botanic Guide to Health (1889)*:

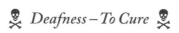

☠ *Deafness – To Cure* ☠

Spirit tincture of lobelia – 1 drachm
Oil of hemlock – 1 drachm
Oil of sassafras – 1 drachm
Oil of wintergreen – 1 drachm
Olive oil – 1 drachm

> *When they are well mixed apply linen wet with the liniment in the ear night and morning; then syringe out with warm water and soap. We have with this liniment cured inveterate cases of deafness.*

PESTICIDES

It was not known that flies spread disease for much of the nineteenth century. However, the amount of horse manure on the streets and the poor sanitation made flies a nuisance. Glass fly traps were used in sick rooms; these had a trough at the base, which was filled with a sugar and water solution, or a milk/water/arsenic solution. Flies could find their way in, but not out, and were eventually drowned or poisoned by the liquid.

Sticky fly papers, which attract flies with their smell and then glue them tight to the paper, were popular. A book of pharmaceutical formulas cites the recipe on the off-chance that 'any retailer is rash enough to wish to manufacture these papers.' Arsenic fly papers were very popular and chemists regularly made up fresh supplies by dipping paper in a prepared solution and hanging them up to dry.

Arsenic Fly Papers

Arsenious acid ℥iv.
Solution of potash ℥xvj.
Sugar lb.ij.
Water Cong.j.

Boil together until the arsenic is dissolved.

FIREWORKS

Prior to the Explosives Act of 1875, there were no controls relating to the sale of gunpowder or fireworks, and there were no lengths to which the pharmacist was not prepared to go to haul in custom. Chemists mixed gunpowder and made fireworks; recipes from the day detail ingredients for a range of firework effects. The recipe for rockets taken from *Charles Wallwork's Receipt Book* of 1830, shown below, is typical in that it does not provide any method for the mixing of the powder, or constructing the packaging.

 *Sky Rockets*

5 oz Salt Petre
10 z Brimstone
10 z Charcoal

Such activities were not without risk, as was reported in *The Chemist &*
Druggist of 15 April 1868. The magazine detailed the sad tale of a chemist's shop
destroyed by an explosion that killed one person and injured two others at 8.45
on a Saturday evening in Nottingham. An errand boy had been employed to
grind 1¾ lb (795 g) of chlorate of potash. It appears that he took the initiative
to add the second ingredient listed, sulphur, despite not having been instructed
to do so. He clearly did not realise the danger of the mix; chlorate of potash
becomes an unstable and explosive material when combined with sulphur.
The unfortunate errand boy pounded once too often and sparked the explosion
that killed him. The verdict was accidental death.

ANIMAL HUSBANDRY

One area that the chemists of the day commonly engaged in, which they do not
today, was the provision of medicines and tonics for animals. The general
thinking appears to have been that if drugs can make us well, they can do the
same for our animals. Boots supplied Liquid for Beekeepers, Foot-Rot Paste
and Mixed Bird Seed. *The Chemist & Druggist* provided its readers with
a regular supply of recipes to deal with ailing livestock.

 *Arsenic-and-sulphur Sheep Dip*

Arsenious acid ℥xij.
Dried sodium carbonate ℥xij.
Sulphur ℥iv.
Mix. For a shilling packet, to make 30 gals. of dip for as many sheep.
Yellow arsenious sulphide may be used instead of whute arsenic.

☠ Liquid medicines for horses ☠

Mild drink (which the horse should take willingly)
Barley Water for inflammatory and catarrhal complaints
Barley 1lb, water 2 gallons, boil to 6 quarts, strain and add 1lb of honey.
If common barley is used it should be first boiled with a little water and
this thrown away. If pearl barley is used this will be less necessary.

☠ Poultry Spice ☠

The following is said to be of assistance to the hens during the laying season:-

Mustard 20 oz
Fenugreek 15 oz
Ground oyster shells 12 oz
Ground bones 8 oz
Sulphate of soda 4 oz
Cayenne pepper 10 oz
Black Antimony 10 oz
Peroxide of iron 10 oz
Corn flour 20 oz
Asafœtida 1 oz

All in powder and mixed.
A teaspoon in the food for a dozen hens
This mixture may be used as a condition powder for poultry generally
when they are out of sorts.

Following page: Pharmacists supplied medicines for animals at a time when good health
and productivity of valueable livestock was crucial for a farmer's survival. ☞

CHAPTER 7

THE APPLIANCES OF SCIENCE

'I firmly believe that if the whole material medica could be sunk to the bottom of the sea, it would be all the better for mankind and all the worse for the fishes.'

OLIVER WENDELL HOLMES, SR. (1809–1894, CELEBRATED AMERICAN PHYSICIAN, PROFESSOR, MEDICAL REFORMER AND AUTHOR)

Developments in medical understanding transformed the treatment of disease during Queen Victoria's 64 years on the throne. In 1875, the Public Health Act comprehensively tackled housing, sewage and drainage, water supply and contagious diseases, and provided Britain with an extensive public health system for the first time. Councils were required to provide clean drinking water and to provide proper sanitation and drainage. This marked the first attempts to tackle the appalling living standards caused by the rapid urban growth of the Industrial Revolution.

But it was scientific developments that led to the most rapid changes in medical treatments. The stethoscope, invented in 1817, was widely used by the mid-century and microscopes had advanced sufficiently to allow the examination of micro-organisms. In the late 1840s, surgery was transformed by the invention of anaesthesia.

The first anaesthetic used was ether: Dr Crawford Long (1815–1878), from Jefferson, Georgia, used it to remove two tumours from a patient's neck in 1842, and the first successful demonstration of its use took place at Massachusetts General Hospital in 1846.

However, it was chloroform that soon became the anaesthetic of choice. Queen Victoria was given chloroform for her eighth delivery, of Prince Leopold in 1853, and for her ninth and final child, Princess Beatrice, in 1857. Her Majesty was anaesthetised by Dr John Snow (1813–1858), also considered one of the fathers

*Early anaesthesia was far from reliable: 1 in 1,500 people died as a direct result
of chloroform anaesthesia, 1 in 15,000 died as a result of being administered ether.
The Maddox inhaler (above) was used for chloroform anaesthesia between 1847 and 1900.*

THE APPLIANCES OF SCIENCE

of epidemiology for his work in identifying the source of a cholera outbreak as a water pump in Broad Street, Soho in 1854.

Germ theory proposed that micro-organisms were the cause of many diseases. The concept was not new, but it was not fully proven until Louis Pasteur (1822–1895) demonstrated that decay was caused by living organisms in the air. He discovered that the bacteria and moulds present in liquids such as wine and milk could be killed by heat treatment – a process now known as pasteurisation. A Glasgow surgeon Joseph Lister (1827–1912) was fascinated by Pasteur's work and recognised that microbes in the air could also cause the putrefaction of wounds.

In the mid-nineteenth century, post-operative sepsis infection accounted for almost 50 per cent of deaths after surgery. Incredible as it may seem, doctors, midwives and surgeons did not wash their hands before treating a patient.

Lister had learnt that carbolic acid was being used to treat sewage in Carlisle and that fields treated with it were freed from a parasite causing death in cattle. He began to sterilise surgical instruments and to clean and dress wounds with a carbolic spray. In 1867, Lister informed the British Medical Association that his wards had been clear of sepsis for nine months. Despite this incontrovertible proof, there was much initial resistance to his theories, but Lister is now recognised as one of the pioneers of infection control. Among his many honours, a mouthwash, Listerine, was named after him in 1879. Infections and deaths fell sharply and this, combined with anaesthesia, allowed surgeons to work more slowly and carefully on their patients, which in turn led to other new discoveries.

In 1879, Robert Koch proved that specific bacteria caused particular diseases. He identified the tuberculosis bacillus in 1882 and followed this up a year later with the discovery of the cholera bacillus. In 1884, Koch's assistant isolated the bacillus responsible for diphtheria, a serious throat infection where the growth of false membranes slowly suffocates the patient.

In just nine years between 1875 and 1884, the bacteria responsible for amoebic dysentery, gonorrhoea, typhoid, leprosy, malaria, tetanus and pneumonia were all identified. With these discoveries, work could begin to discover how the diseases were spread and how they could be prevented and treated, promoting extensive public health campaigns.

Surgeon James Young Simpson and his friends sampled new chemicals to see if they had any anaesthetic effect, as this illustration from the 1840s reveals. Simpson discovered the anaesthetic use of chloroform; 30,000 mourners lined the streets of Edinburgh for his funeral.

DISINFECTION

In *Disinfection and Disinfectants* (1895), Dr Samuel Rideal explained:

> *The ideal of disinfection is to stamp out the pathogenic bacteria, just as weeds are extirpated from a garden. This can never be done until their hotbeds, the filthy slums of the cities and the neglected country villages, are cleansed, supplied with plenty of good water, and, in the cities, with air and, above all, light. Every dirty court or alley is an admirable*

culture-medium in which disease organisms may multiply; these issuing in a variety of ways, as by clothes, food, and even sometimes by the atmosphere, may unexpectedly decimate the so-called better neighbourhoods.

In line with this, chemists were manufacturing their own cleaning and disinfecting materials, encouraging the public to take care of their health by killing germs. The working men and women of London did not have the time or the wherewithal to make their own cleaning materials, as the farmer's wife might have done.

 *Carbolic Soap*

Say 1 and a quarter pounds of tallow or lard
1½ pounds of common soda
7 ounces of rosin
4 ounces of stone lime
1 ounce of palm oil

Dissolve the Soda and Lime in one quart of water. Boil until all is melted stirring well. Remove from the fire and allow the mixture to settle, afterwards pouring off the clear lye from the top and boiling therein the tallow, rosin and palm oil. Boil gently until the mixture becomes a pasty substance, then take off the fire and add four tablespoons of carbolic acid, pour in a box to cool, throw over the box a piece of coarse canvas so as to retain the strength of the acid while cooling. The same carbolic acid is used as that sold for disinfecting.

The disinfectant which best satisfied scientific requirements in the destruction of micro-organisms was known as the 'English Local Government Board's Solution'. This was recommended to local Boards of Health during the 1892 cholera scare:

CROSFIELD'S SOAP WORKS.

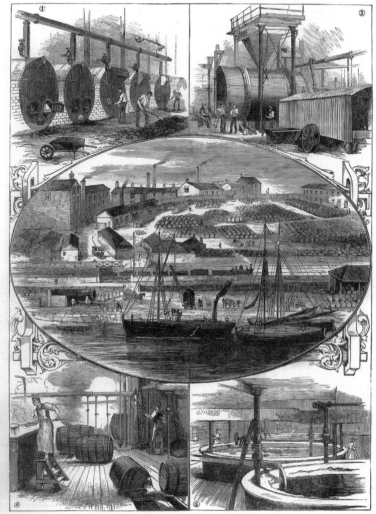

1. View in the Boiler Shed.   2. A glimpse of the Alkali Plant.   3. The Raw Material as it arrives in the Mersey in Casks.   4. The Raw Material being melted out of the Casks.   5. A few of the Pans.

Pharmacists could, and did, make their own soap, however as production became increasingly industrialised it became a product they could buy in. Crosfield's Soap Works in Warrington, pictured here in 1886, was acquired by Lever Brothers in 1919.

☠ *Disinfectant* ☠

Corrosive sublimate ℥ss
Hydrochloric acid ℥j
Aniline blue gr. v
Water Cong. iij.

If a family was struck by an infectious disease, the advice was to immerse all clothes and bedclothes in a disinfectant solution. This could be purchased as a powder or as compressed tablets, which the customer could dissolve in the required measures of water at home. Jeyes Disinfectant was invented by John Jeyes (1817–1892) in 1877 and his firm was granted a Royal Warrant in 1896.

Another disinfectant was sulphur. Sulphur candles were made by fusing sulphur, pouring it into a mould and placing a wick in the centre. Anyone wanting to do-it-themselves was advised to place an iron receptacle in a pan of water – to help prevent fire. Some ¾ lb (340 g) of ordinary sulphur was required for every 500 cubic feet (14 cubic metres) of space. Doors and windows were to be sealed, using cloth or paper where there were draughts. Methylated spirit was poured on the sulphur to help it light, then the door was closed and left for at least six hours.

Fumigating powders for use in sick rooms were made by dipping sheets of blotting paper into a solution of potassium nitrate and boiling water. This was hung up and dried, then sprayed with an appropriate mix of perfumes.

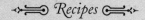

❧ *Recipes* ❧

Rose Soap

This soap is very fragrant, and is one of the finest toilet soaps.

Common white soap 30 lbs
Olive oil soap 20 lbs
Vermillion powder 1½ oz
Oil of rose 3 oz
Oil of cinnamon 1 oz
Oil of cloves 1 oz
Oil of bergamot 2 oz

Cut the soaps into thin pieces and place in a pan with 2 gallons of boiling water. Allow the soap to remain on the heat until thoroughly melted; remove from the heat and add the vermillion powder. After the soap has cooled a little, stir in the essential oils. Pour into boxes or moulds.

PURITAN
SOAP

FAIRY
HOUSEHOLD SOAP

HT

BROOKES
MONKEY

By-products of the mining industry – tars, oils and gases – were used in the creation of Izal disinfectant in 1893, one of the best-known brands. It was available as a liquid, a powder, soap and ointment.

Toilet tissue was first commercially manufactured in America by Joseph Gayetty in 1857. The product contained aloe, and Gayetty's name was printed on every sheet. Advertising declared it as 'The greatest necessity of the age! Gayetty's medicated paper for the water-closet.' Production did not come to England until the British Perforated Paper Company began selling boxes of pre-cut squares in 1880. It was very coarse, but prior to this it was common to use torn-up bits of newspaper. Perforated paper was generally medicated, and came in packs of 100 or 500 individual sheets; a patent for a continuous toilet roll was taken out in 1870 by the Scott Brothers of Philadelphia. Toilet paper was an unmentionable product for many years, and was sold wrapped in brown paper for discretion.

☠ *Disinfecting Liquid* ☠

Put two pints of water into a bottle and add

Acetate of lead 2 oz.
Strong Nitric acid 2 fluid oz.

Shake the mix together vigorously and use dilute to clean floors and surfaces.

CLEANING PRODUCTS

Doing the laundry was regarded as one of the worst household chores: it was heavy, exhausting work. Washing machines were not invented until the 1880s and even then they were very basic, often tearing clothes or leaving them marked. In *The Complete Home; An Encyclopaedia of Domestic Life and Affairs* (1879), Julia McNair Wright points describes washing as 'a great burden and often a family bugbear.' McNair Wright advises women: 'Remember that washing is very hard work; more young women break down their strength with washing than any other toil.' She points out that young women should not mix work with washing:

> … if they would lighten the task by soaking the clothes, and by using a clothes wringer … instead of straining their chests and ruining their backs by lifting tubs of water, or boilers of clothes, or by carrying to the line a basket heaped with wet clothes … we should have fewer broken-down women.

Borax was a commonly used cleaner. This naturally occurring mineral has many uses as a natural laundry booster, multi-purpose cleaner, fungicide, preservative, insecticide, herbicide and disinfectant, and has the advantage of mixing with most other cleaning agents:

☠ *Borax Soap Powder* ☠

> *Soap 5lbs*
> *Soda 3lbs*
> *Silicate of soda 2lbs*
> *Borax 1lb*

> *The best soap to use is made up of equal parts of tallow [animal fat] and cocoa-nut oil. Slice the soap and put it into a steam bath with its own weight of water. When it is nearly melted, put in a little of the soda which helps to make the last of the soap melt. Then add the rest of the soda and stir until completely dissolved.*

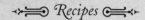

Antibacterial Cleaner

A quick and easy household cleaner.

———•◆•———

Malt vinegar 10 ½ fl oz
Lemon juice 5 fl oz
Gum arabic to taste

Pour the malt vinegar and lemon juice into a bottle and shake to combine. If you want a thick consistency, then a little gum arabic (a food often used in sweets) will do the job.

Lavender Water

Use as a fragrant spray when ironing.

———•◆•———

Vodka 1 –2 teaspoons
Lavender oil 6 drops

Put the vodka into a glass and add the lavender oil, mix until the oil is dispersed. Put 7 fl oz water into a sprinkler or spray bottle, add the alcohol mix and shake vigorously.

Put the mix onto a galvanised iron tin in a well ventilated area and keep moving it so that the mixture does not separate. Add the rest of the ingredients and keep moving the mixture until it has become quite thick. Put on one side for one or two days until it is quite hard and crunchy and can be broken up. Grind into a fine powder in a mill.

Clothes washed in soap powder were inclined to become yellow. So, to achieve a whiter-than-white finish laundry, blue powder, or Dolly Blue bags, were used. The powder could be popped into a homemade bag of flannel or muslin – if it wasn't supplied with one – and stirred around in the final rinse. Commercially made brands, such as Reckitt's Paris Blue Squares, cost a penny an ounce. It came with the following recommendation from Eliza Elder in 1873: 'I have been laundress to the Prince of Wales for several years, and I consider Reckitt's Paris blue is the best I ever used, and is undoubtedly greatly superior to the old-fashioned thumb or dark blue.' *The Chemist & Druggist*, however, urged its readers to take advantage of the enormous demand for laundry blue and make their own.

☠ *Thumb or Table Blue* ☠

Superfine ultramarine ℥iv.
Ordinary ultramarine ℥ij.
Sodium carbonate ℥iv.
Glucose ℥ix.

Mix and make into a stiff paste by the aid of water, roll out into a thick sheet, and cut into cubes which dry at a gentle heat.

Chemists were also encouraged to try to sell bleaching agents, which the *The Chemist & Druggist* advised were 'very popular on the continent'.

 *Eau de Javelle*

Chlorinated lime ℥iij.
Pearl ash ℥iij.
Water Oiv.
Hydrochloric acid ℥ij.

Mix the lime with Oiiiss. of water, and dissolve the pearl ash in the remainder; mix, and after a few days filter, add the hydrochloric acid to the filtrate.

Clothing was washed infrequently, so the removal of grease spots was something of an obsession. Chemists were well versed in the science of stain removal, whether grease, gunpowder, coffee, iron, milk, wax or ink and whether on linen, silk or wool. Lightening renovators could be used on wool, black clothes, carpets and, indeed, windows – users were advised to keep the product away from naked flames, as it contained rectified spirit, ether and ammonia. Keeping buttons shiny and household silver gleaming was another task for which the chemist provided products. He sold silver soap, gilding paste and even a paste made specially to clean policeman's buttons:

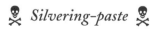 *Silvering-paste*

Tin dust ℥j.
Mercury ℥iv.

Run together until an amalgam is formed, use as required.

 *Silver Plate Powders*

Precipitated chalk ℥viij.

Spirit of turpentine ℥ij.

Spirit ℥j.

Spirit of camphor ℥ss.

Solution of ammonia ℥ij.

Mix the powder into a paste and use as required.

QUACKS AND MACHINERY

Scientific developments led to the development of all manner of weird and wacky machines: medical men were genuinely interested in how the understanding of oxygen, electricity and X-rays could benefit their patients, while opportunists recognised the lucrative potential of the market. Either way, most of the machines promised much and delivered little.

Oxygen therapy, or diaduction, was a concept that interested the public. Its early use was neither rational nor scientific; it was touted as a panacea by quacks and was sold in pharmacies and chemists. Converts could purchase oxygenated water, or oxygen to be inhaled. Dr Samuel S Wallian, writing in 1886, observed:

> *Most of these advertisers name their 'secret' preparation 'compound oxygen'. As to their nature, all are about alike; and it ought to be unnecessary to repeat to intelligent physicians that none of them contain free oxygen … that these solutions are useful is quintessence of bosh. The exercise of a grain of chemical common sense will render all this pretentious nonsense.*

The Oxydonor Victory was invented by Dr Hercule Sanche, a notorious quack from Detroit, Michigan; he patented the device in 1890. Sanche claimed that, by forcing oxygen into the body via a special pump, it was possible to 'cure all form of Disease quickly, intangibly, pleasantly, infallibly, during sleep or while awake; and to brace the human system in all conditions, with Animation never known and not otherwise attained, whether in Disease, Debility, or in

Fatigue, and in all Physical and Mental Ordeals.' The user placed metal plates of copper or aluminium on their body with bands. Wires led from these to a nickel- or chrome-plated sealed cylinder, which the user placed in a bowl of water. The cylinder was sometimes empty and sometimes contained a carbon rod. Devices such as these were known as gas pipes – and they did nothing.

Sold between 1890 and around 1910, Macaura's Pulsocon Vibrating Massager, later renamed Macaura's Blood Circulator, was advertised as curing rheumatism, neuralgia, lumbago, 'chest problems' and other maladies by the means of vibratory massage. The device, about 12 in (30 cm) long, featured a vibrating pad, which was activated when a handle was turned. The vibrations, 2,000 per minute, were surprisingly intense, but in 1913 'Dr' Macaura was sentenced to jail for three years for impersonating a doctor and for fraudulent advertising.

Electricity was a new and novel force in the nineteenth century. Numerous quack devices were developed in the name of 'electrotherapy' and were used indiscriminately. Davis & Kidders Patent Electro-Magnetic machine 'for nervous diseases' was patented in 1854 and continued to sell until around 1890. The device generated an electric current from a hand crank – the faster the crank was turned, the stronger the current. Two rotating magnets, in close proximity to each other, produced the current, which was transferred to the patient via wires and metal handles. Patients felt high voltage electric shocks coursing throughout the body and were left afterwards with a buzzing sensation – which, some claimed, relieved their symptoms.

Isaac Pulvermacher, a Prussian, came to England and worked as a medical battery maker. He created Pulvermacher's Medical Electric Chains and claimed to have:

thousands of Testimonials from Clergymen, Barristers, Naval and Military Officers & others, show that one of these chains cure, without pain, trouble, or any other medicine, all kinds of Rheumatic, Neuralgic, Epileptic, Paralytic, & Nervous Complaints, Indigestion, Spasms & a host of others. No remedy ever discovered has attracted such high praise as this. Philosophers, divines, eminent physicians, in all parts of the world, recommend them. Effects instant and agreeable. May be tested beforehand. Price 5s and 10s 6d.

Pulvermacher's Electric Belts went a step further: they featured an electric chain in a belt connected to a 'suspensory' for a man's 'vitals'. The device was designed to cure everything from impotence to 'debilities of sexual self pollution'. The devices supposedly supplied 'mild continuous currents' for 8–12 hours. They were then immersed in a weak vinegar solution to recharge.

The Electric Corset, sold by Cornelius Bennett Harness, was actually magnetic rather than electric. Initially he distributed Dr Scott's Electric Corset from America, but then decided to manufacture his own. Harness claimed it had marvellous health-giving properties: 'it invigorates the entire system and assists nature in the Healthy Development of the Chest.' Harness also offered 'electropathic' belts. Containing zinc and copper plates, these were supposed to generate a health-giving current and generate new life and vigour in weak men and women.

The Electro-static Eliminator maintained that it reduced static to 'normal' and that it should be used nightly for two weeks. It claimed it could cure everything from gout and lumbago to dysentery, 'women's diseases', diabetes and many more. All of these devices were enormously popular for a while, but by the turn of the century the public had become disillusioned with them. Reputable machinery was confined to use by doctors. The modern equivalent is the TENS machine, which is used for pain relief in rheumatism and labour, and for muscles stimulation in the pelvic area.

Not all inventions were nonsense. In November 1895, the German physicist Wilhelm Röntgen (1845–1923) discovered the see-through properties of X-rays. The medical significance of the discovery was realised immediately, and it was rapidly put to use in America to reveal the position of a bullet in a patient's leg. Within six months, hospitals were installing X-ray machines. The benefits were transparent, but newspapers, ever on the alert for a good story, suggested that X-rays were an affront to female decency.

An oil painting by Edmund Bristow from 1824 shows the dispensing of medical electricity.

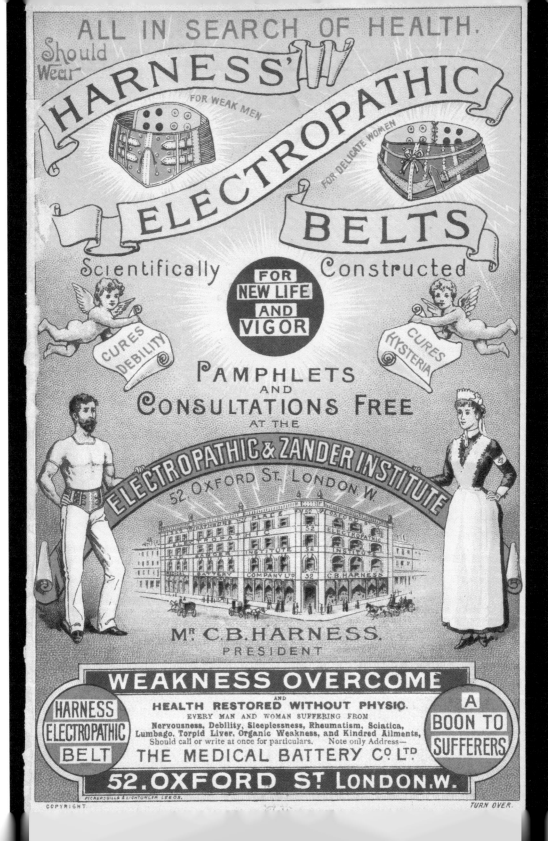

The result was a short-lived range of X-ray proof underwear, launched to protect feminine virtue. The discovery of radiation followed in 1896 and, with it, the hope of a treatment for cancer.

THE TRIUMPH OF SCIENCE

By the end of the Victorian era, we find the beginnings of attempts to insist that products lived up to their claims. Jesse Boot may have started out with no pharmaceutical experience, but he understood and appreciated the benefits that trained pharmacists could offer. In 1895 he opened the Analytical Department, which examined every product sold in Boots from the raw materials of its own products, to the proprietary brand names from other manufacturers. In one year, an astonishing 71 per cent of the samples analysed were below the standards demanded by Boots and therefore the products were rejected.

By 1900, pharmaceutical manufacturers were turning discoveries made in university laboratories to profit. This included Henry Wellcome (1853–1926), who started life as a travelling salesman peddling pills; and Silas Burroughs (1853–1936), who was the first American to bring mass-produced pills to Britain. Together they formed Burroughs, Wellcome and Co in 1879, and by 1882 they were manufacturing their own drugs and taking the first steps toward liberating the Victorian pharmacist from the daily grind of pill making. Henry Wellcome invented the brand name 'Tabloid' and they applied it to all of their products, from their compressed tablets, to cosmetics, tea and photographic-developing chemicals.

By 1900, the medical advances were substantial, from the discovery of aspirin and the invention of X-rays, to the development of germ theory. The profession had matured, and fluke remedies and quack potions were being replaced as new scientific understanding paved the way for inventions and products that actually worked. The Victorian pharmacist had come of age.

An advertisement for Harness' Electropathic Belts which claimed to cure hysteria, nervousness, sleeplessness, rheumatism, sciatica, lumbago and torpid livers!

BIBLIOGRAPHY

ANDERSON, Stuart, ed. *Making Medicines*. Pharmaceutical Press: 2005

BYNUM, W.F. and PORTER, Roy, eds. *Medical Fringe and Medical Orthodoxy 1750–1850*. Croom Helm Ltd: 1987

CHAPMAN, Stanley. *Jesse Boot of Boots The Chemist*. Hodder and Stoughton: 1974

CHURCH, Roy and TANSEY, E.M. Burroughs Wellcome & Co. *Transformation of the British Pharmaeceutical Industry*. Crucible Books: 2007

ENRIGHT, D.J., ed. *The Faber Book of Fevers and Frets*. Faber and Faber: 1989

FOX, William. *The Working Man's Model Botanic Guide to Health*. William Fox: 1889.

GORDON, Richard. *Ailments through the Age*. Michael O Mara Books Ltd: 1997

GRANSHAW, Lindsay and PORTER, Roy, eds. *The Hospital in History*. Routledge: 1989

GRAY, Linda. *Grow Your Own Pharmacy*. Findhorn Press: 2007

HARDY, Anne. *Health and Medicine in Britain since 1860*. Palgrave: 2001

HILL CURTH, Louise, ed. *From Physick to Pharmacology*. Ashgate: 2006

HOMAN, Peter G.; HUDSON Briony; and ROWE Raymond C. *Popular Medicines*. Pharmaceutical Press: 2008

KELP-PHILIP, Robert. *Victorian Family Save-All*. Marquis de Fosseway: 1861

LEWIS, Dulcie. *The A-Z of Traditional Cures & Remedies*. Countryside Books: 2002

MACEWAN, Peter. *Pharmaceutical Formulas – A Book of Useful Recipes for the Drug Trade*. Publisher unknown: 1898

MATHISON, Richard. *The Eternal Search*. G.P. Putnam's Sons: 1958

MATTHEWS, Leslie G. *History of Pharmacy in Britain*. E&S Livingstone Ltd: 1962

PORTER, Roy. *Quacks*. Tempus: 2000

PORTER, Roy. *Blood & Guts*. Penguin: 2002

PORTER, Dorothy and PORTER Roy. *Patient's Progress*. Polity Press: 1989

STRATHERN, Paul. *A Brief History of Medicine*. Robinson: 2005

WHORTON, James C. *The Arsenic Century*. Oxford University Press: 2010

WONG, James. *Grow Your Own Drugs*. Collins: 2009

YOUNG, Anne Mortimer. *Antique Medicine Chests*. Vernier Press: 1994

Enquire Within upon Everything. Herbert Jenkins Ltd: 1890

INDEX

ACKNOWLEDGEMENTS

A huge thank you to Lion TV for their confidence in me and particularly to Cassie Braban, David Upshal, Gillian Pauling, Laura Rawlinson, Nick Catliff and Richard Shaw for their invaluable help in preparing this book. Staff at the library and museum of The Royal Pharmaceutical Society of Great Britain were generous with their time and advice and Briony Hudson answered my many queries with boundless patience. Sophie Clapp at Boots was tremendously helpful and made exploring the fascinating Boots archive a great pleasure. Our local chemist James Milne, now retired, helped me understand some technical details and made some fascinating archive material available. My children Florence, Teddy and Genevieve showed their usual patience as I related endless gruesome pharmaceutical tales for their edification and my husband Eric deserves thanks for maintaining his nerve despite my grisly bedtime reading matter on the use of arsenic and the murder trials of Victorian poisoners. Finally I would like to thank Polly Powell, Anna Cheifetz, Katie Deane, Julian Alexander, Chris Terry and Kate Ward for their faith in me and for all their support in the production of this book.

Above, from left to right: Cassie Braban, Gillian Pauling and David Upshal. Below: the team at Lion television filming on location. Overleaf: further scenes being filmed both inside and outside of the pharmacy.

Picture Credits

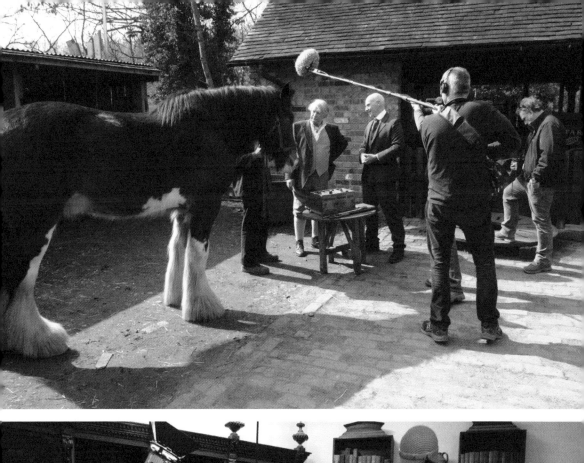

Recipe Sources

Page 18: Blistering Ointment (*The Chemist & Druggist* 15th September 1884)

Page 19: Lemon Wash Balls (*The Druggist's General Receipt Book*, Henry Beasley, 10th Edition 1895)

Page 25: First Aid Kit (*Victorian Farm*, Anova Books, 2009 Edition)

Page 25: Oil of Earthworms (Old herbal remedy, source unknown)

Page 29: Stramonium (*Companion to the British Pharmacoepia* of 1864)

Page 29: Oat Bath (Old herbal remedy, source unknown)

Page 29: Chamomile Bath (Old herbal remedy, source unknown)

Page 31: Essence of Blackberry (*Manual of Formulæ*, 1892 Published at the Offices of The British And Colonial Druggist)

Page 35: Curry Powder (*Manual of Formulæ*, 1892 Published at the Offices of The British And Colonial Druggist)

Page 41: Insect Preventative (*Manual of Formulæ*, 1892 Published at the Offices of The British And Colonial Druggist)

Page 49: Bergamot Tea (Old herbal remedy, source unknown)

Page 51: Gargyle, Anti-syphilitic (*Manual of Formulæ*, 1892 Published at the Offices of The British And Colonial Druggist)

Page 51: Dill Water (Old herbal remedy, source unknown)

Page 53: Tarragon Digestive (Old herbal remedy, source unknown)

Page 55: Beef Tea (*The Druggist's General Receipt Book*, by Henry Beasley, 1895)

Page 59: Chervil Water (Old herbal remedy, source unknown)

Page 59: Chamomile Rinse (Old herbal remedy, source unknown)

Page 63: Rosemary Water (Old herbal remedy, source unknown)

Page 65: Popular Remedy for consumption (*The Druggist's General Receipt Book*, by Henry Beasley, 1895)

Page 67: Sprain Oil (*Rickets Family archive*)

Page 73: Oatmeal Paste (Old herbal remedy, source unknown)

Page 74: Instantaneous Toothache-Cure (*The Chemist & Druggist* 30th January 1892)

Page 75: Liquid Dentifrice (*Manual of Formulæ*, 1892 Published at the Offices of The British And Colonial Druggist)

Page 79: Fennel Tea (Old herbal remedy, source unknown)

Page 79: Peppermint Tea (Old herbal remedy, source unknown)

Page 80: British Herbal Tobacco (*The Druggist's General Receipt Book*, by Henry Beasley, 1895)

Page 81: Hair Oil (*Manual of Formulæ*, 1892 Published at the Offices of The British And Colonial Druggist)

Page 83: Marshmallow Lotion (Old herbal remedy, source unknown)

Page 85: Ointment for Ringworm (*The Chemist & Druggist* 15th May 1884)

Page 85: Custard Powder (*Manual of Formulæ*, 1892 Published at the Offices of The British And Colonial Druggist)

Page 87: Opium Soothing Drink (*The Chemist & Druggist* 15th September 1884)

Page 87: Children's cough Syrup (*Pharmaceutical Journal Formulary* 1915)

Page 89: Diarrhœa Mixture (*Chemists' Annual and Diary*)

Page 89: Lovage Infusion (Old herbal remedy, source unknown)

Page 89: Peppermint Tisane (Old herbal remedy, source unknown)

Pages 90/91: Pharmacist Colours (*The Chemist & Druggist Pharmaceutical Formulas* from 1898)

Page 91: Liquid Rouge (*The Druggist General Receipt Book*, Beasley, 10th edition 1895)

Page 97: Soothing Syrup or Mother's Friend (*The Working Man's Model Botanic Guide to Health*)

Page 101: Elderflower Ointment (*The Book of Receipts*, Lucas, 11th edition 1907)

Page 104: Sage and Vinegar Poultice (Old herbal remedy, source unknown)

Page 109: Dandruff Lotion (*Manual of Formulæ*, 1892 Published at the Offices of The British And Colonial Druggist)

Page 109: Nettle Hair Rinse (Old herbal remedy, source unknown)

Page 115: Peppermint Lozenges (*The Druggist's General Receipt Book*, by Henry Beasley, 1895)

Page 119: Love Hearts (*Victorian Farm*, Anova Books, 2009 Edition)

Page 121: Witch Hazel Cream (*The Book of Receipts*, Lucas, 11th edition 1907)

Page 124: Chlorodyne (*The Druggist's General Receipt Book*, by Henry Beasley, 1895)

Page 133: Almond Wash Powder (*The Druggist's General Receipt Book*, by Henry Beasley, 1895)

Page 137: Perspiration Powder (*The Druggist General Receipt Book*, Beasley, 10th edition 1895)

Page 141: Cold Cream (Old herbal remedy, source unknown)

Page 144: Cachou Aromatise (*Pharmaceutical Formulas*)

Page 145: Marshmallow Milk (Old herbal remedy, source unknown)

Page 147: Horseradish Syrup (Old herbal remedy, source unknown)

Page 151: Bread Poultice (Old herbal remedy, source unknown)

Page 151: Mustard Poultice (Old herbal remedy, source unknown)

Page 153: Rose Freckle Lotion (*Pharmaceutical Formulas*)

Page 155: German Lip Salve (*The Druggist's General Receipt Book*, by Henry Beasley, 1895)

Page 155: Cheap Pomade (*The Chemist & Druggist* 16 April 1892)

Page 157: Floral Perfume (Old herbal remedy, source unknown)

Page 157: A Light Summer Perfume (Old herbal remedy, source unknown)

Page 159: Eau de Cologne No 1 (*Chemical Recipes* The Atlas Chemical Company,1896)

Page 165: Browning Sauce (*Pharmaceutical Formulas*)

Page 166: Blancmange Powder (*Pharmaceutical Formulas*)

Page 167: Milk Lemonade (*Chemical Recipes* by the Atlas Chemical Company, 1896)

Page 170: Lemon Squash Essence (*Pharmaceutical Formulas*)

Page 170: Lemon Kali (*Pharmaceutical Formulas*)

Page 171: Lemon Verbena tea (Old herbal remedy, source unknown)

Page 173: Tomato Sauce (*Manual of Formulæ*, 1892 Published at the Offices of The British And Colonial Druggist)

Page 179: Arsenic Fly Papers (*Pharmaceutical Formulas*)

Page 180: Arsenic-and-Sulphur Sheep Dip (*Pharmaceutical Formulas*)

Page 190: Carbolic Soap *(Chemical Recipes* by The Atlas Chemical Company, 1896)

Page 192: Corrosive Sublimate (*Pharmaceutical Formulas*)

Page 193: Rose Soap (*Chemical Recipes* by the Atlas Chemical Company, 1896)

Page 196: Disinfecting Liquid (Old herbal remedy, source unknown)

Page 197: Borax Soap Powder (*Pharmaceutical Formulas*)

Page 197: Antibacterial Cleaner (*Victorian Farm*, Anova Books, 2009 Edition)

Page 197: Lavender Water (Old herbal remedy, source unknown)

Page 199: Silvering Paste (*Pharmaceutical Formulas*)

Page 199: Silver Plate Powders (*Pharmaceutical Formulas*)

First published in the United Kingdom
in 2010 by Pavilion,
an imprint of Anova Books,
10 Southcombe Street,
London, W14 0RA

Produced in association with Lion Television Ltd, 26 Paddenswick Road,
London, W6 0UB

Programme and Format © Lion Television, 2010
Foreword © Ruth Goodman, 2010
Design and text © Pavilion, 2010

Associate Publisher: Anna Cheifetz
Project Editor: Katie Deane
Copy Editor: Caroline Curtis
Proofreader: Kathy Steer
Indexer: Patricia Hyman
Designer: Kate Ward
Cover Designer: Georgina Hewitt
Production Manager: Oliver Jeffreys
Anova Photographer: Chris Terry
Lion Television Photographer: Laura Rawlinson
(See Picture Credits, page 214, for further copyright information.)

The moral rights of the author have been asserted.
A CIP catalogue record for this book is available from the British Library.

10 9 8 7 6 5 4 3 2 1

ISBN 978-1-86205-890-3

Reproduction by Rival Colour Limited, UK
Printed by L.E.G.O. spa, Italy.
www.anovabooks.com

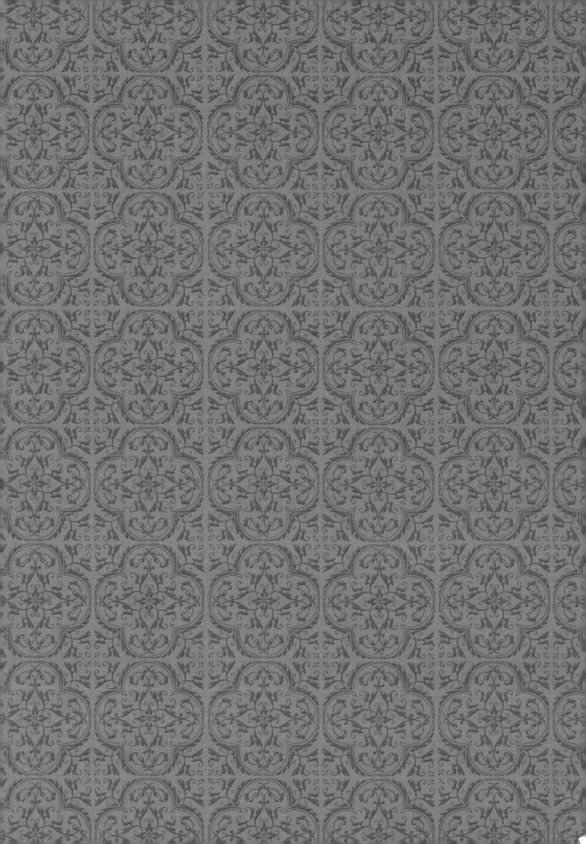